Advance Praise for *Libera...*

"What could be a more worthy goal than creating wise schools? *Liberating Leadership Capacity* strikes a chord with those who believe that education is more than a series of tasks and tests, and that curiosity, wonder, and emerging leadership should define the experiences of students and teachers alike."

—Deborah Walker, president and CEO, Collaborative for Teaching and Learning (CTL)

"Leadership is widely regarded as a key ingredient of school success, and in this important and informative new book the work done by innovative educational leaders is carefully analyzed and explored. The insights conveyed are profound and should be shared with educators and policymakers who seek to help schools make a difference for children— particularly those from the most disadvantaged backgrounds—and our society. Written in clear and accessible language, it is an invaluable resource for anyone seeking to understand how to address the many challenges facing our nation's schools."

—Pedro A. Noguera, distinguished professor of education, UCLA Graduate School of Education & Information Studies

"Liberating Leadership Capacity teaches us not only how to think about systemwide change but how it is developed and what it looks like in practice. At last we have a authoritative text on how to organize trusting relationships, knowledge development, and collaboration as principals and teachers take on the leadership challenge together."

—Ann Lieberman, senior scholar at Stanford University

"In Liberating Leadership Capacity, a compelling driving concept is that 'leadership capacities are present in the room.' The authors describe organizational conditions that promote skillful dialogue, continual learning, building trust, and sharing a common vision among members. In such schools teachers become the leaders of learning and students become the leaders of the future."

—Arthur L. Costa, professor emeritus, California State University, Sacramento

"In this accessible and comprehensive examination of leadership and leadership capacity, Linda Lambert and her colleagues have cleverly woven together the major themes of scholarship in leadership practice over the past quarter century. In defining and developing their concept of constructivist leadership, they have designed a model that is at once sustainable, distributive, ecological, and transformational. It is an approach that connects with Dewey and the finest traditions of American democracy and stands in stark contrast to market-based leadership models that view professional educators as human capital. I would recommend it as a must-read for anyone interested in dynamic, creative, and inviting schools and school systems."

—Dean Fink, author and consultant

"This visionary book is grounded in practice. The authors bring unique, forthright insights into the deep links between strategies and structures for leading adaptive organizations and the historic ideals of democratizing learning, teaching, and leading within school communities. The offering is a "systems" framework for leading—drawn from national and international perspectives—showing how we are liberated by connective thinking and co-constructing knowledge."

—David Hyerle, codirector, *Thinking Schools International*

"Liberating Leadership Capacity is a refreshing alternative and counternarrative to the constraints of the past and the depleting testing focus educators are confronting. Follow this guide to creating a culture that allows staff, students, parents, and, ultimately, the leaders who set it all in motion to flourish, and you will find a sustainable and systemic path to continued success for every student."

—Alan M. Blankstein, founder, Solution Tree and HOPE Foundation;
author, *Failure Is Not an Option*

LIBERATING LEADERSHIP CAPACITY

Pathways to Educational Wisdom

Linda Lambert
Diane P. Zimmerman
Mary E. Gardner

Foreword by Andy Hargreaves

TEACHERS COLLEGE PRESS

TEACHERS COLLEGE | COLUMBIA UNIVERSITY
NEW YORK AND LONDON

Published by Teachers College Press, 1234 Amsterdam Avenue, New York, NY 10027

Library of Congress Cataloging-in-Publication Data

Names: Lambert, Linda, 1939- author. | Zimmerman, Diane P., author. | Gardner, Mary E. (Educational consultant)
Title: Liberating leadership capacity : pathways to educational wisdom / Linda Lambert, Diane P. Zimmerman, Mary E. Gardner ; foreword by Andy Hargreaves.
Description: New York, NY : Teachers College Press, 2016. | Includes bibliographical references and index.
Identifiers: LCCN 2015048588 (print) | LCCN 2016010240 (ebook) | ISBN 9780807757512 (pbk. : alk. paper) | ISBN 9780807774786 (ebook)
Subjects: LCSH: Educational leadership—United States. | Teacher participation in administration—United States. | School improvement programs—United States.
Classification: LCC LB2805 .L284 2016 (print) | LCC LB2805 (ebook) | DDC 371.2—dc23
LC record available at http://lccn.loc.gov/2015048588

ISBN 978-0-8077-5751-2 (paper)
ISBN 978-0-8077-7478-6 (ebook)

Printed on acid-free paper
Manufactured in the United States of America

23 22 21 20 19 18 17 16   8 7 6 5 4 3 2 1

*We lovingly dedicate this book to the memory of Maxine Greene,
philosopher, artist, educator, writer, and pioneering woman.*

In 1994, when we wrote our first book, *The Constructivist Leader*,
Maxine generously composed the Foreword. She noted that by
eloquently celebrating the democratization of leadership, the
"constructivist leader" was one who engaged self and others in
reciprocal, purposeful learning within community. Leadership, she
further noted, no longer meant taking charge, directing, commanding,
and subjugating others.

Two complementary concepts played vital roles in her development
as the woman who became recognized as the most important American
philosopher since John Dewey. The first concept was that of an
intentional and enlightened philosophy of being. The second concept
suggested how consciousness could be awakened in others as well as the
self. This awakening, or releasing of the imagination, defines learning in
its most powerful forms. Her belief that ideas worth learning have the
capacity to be awakened permeates *Liberating Leadership Capacity*. We
share an understanding with Maxine of the major goal of education: to
nurture intellectual talents for the formation of our society into a more
democratic, just, and caring place.

Democracy, Maxine insisted, is a way of life that recognizes the
capacity of each individual to choose, to act, to construct his or her
own life—to lead. "The wonderful part about being a teacher," she once
said, "is that we can free people to move toward an achievement of their
own freedom, of their own expression, of their own pain, of their own
hopes." We hope that this book provides such a path toward liberation.

Contents

Foreword: Leadership for Liberation

It is an odd thing about leadership that sometimes there is a glaring inconsistency between its goals and means—between what leadership is supposed to achieve and how leadership goes about achieving it. It is a strange system that dictates the imposition of democracy, forces people to be free, or compels them to be creative. Yet in education and elsewhere these leadership inconsistencies occur over and over again. Teachers are given little say in the multiple surveys they have to administer to monitor levels of student engagement. There is an effort to solicit greater student voice but in ways that silence or suppress teachers' voices. Teachers are excluded from decisions about policies that enforce student inclusion. They are made to continue teaching the test while also being chastised for failing to develop 21st-century skills.

Sometimes, there is an argument for top-down leadership—where students are in danger, where existing capacity to improve is limited, or where the goals of education are narrow and specific, such as improving measurable achievements in literacy and mathematics. But the pursuit of narrow goals and limited solutions has run its course, the scope for squeezing a few more percentage points out of conventional attainment scores has diminished, and in countries like England, Sweden and the United States, the costs to teacher recruitment and retention of a system that exposes teachers to unwarranted criticism for the failures of their students have become apparent for the public as well as the profession to see. It is time, Lambert and her colleagues say in this book, to rid ourselves of "the tyranny of serial edicts".

In the volatile and sometimes violent world in which our students are now being educated, the pursuit of higher scores in basic skills remains important but is still not enough; and the means by which we have pursued even that improvement has had questionable success. Two of the countries where standardized testing has been enforced most relentlessly—the United States and England—are now among the world's lowest-performing developed economies in literacy skills at ages 16–19.

The times in which we live are ones defined by great economic uncertainty. The stock market pitches back and forth. Youth unemployment levels have skyrocketed all across Europe. Energy-based economies are collapsing in Canada and the Middle East. American jobs are holding up, but the wages for them are not. The portfolio life of combining different jobs that was once a middle class privilege—think part-time teaching and photography, or business consulting and writing—is now an unenviable working class necessity, returning to the days when people like my widowed mother had to work three jobs like child minding, house cleaning, and shop work just to make ends meet. How do we educate our young people to survive in and help transform these brittle economic realities?

Alongside economic uncertainty is local and global insecurity. Violence against the African American community, including from the very people who are supposed to protect that community, is running amok in U.S. cities. The evils of global terrorism are met with national waves of Islamophobia. Our schools increasingly segregate classes and races instead of bringing them together. Epidemics of gun violence are a symbol and symptom of a society in which young people are increasingly alienated and isolated in and from their communities. How do we teach young people and their families not only what to know and be able to do, but also how to be and how to live together?

Our school systems are now being challenged to address these more complex needs and sophisticated goals. In places like Norway, Scotland, and Ontario in Canada, the prime drivers of reform are no longer simply basic skills and high school graduation rates. They focus on developing confident learners and responsible citizens and on student wellbeing, deeper learning, and creativity. The United States is going to have to keep up—not just for an elite few who will keep on driving innovation in the country's most prestigious universities and business hubs, but also throughout the whole society.

More sophisticated learning requires more sophisticated teaching and leadership. Complex professional judgments cannot be prescribed, standardized, or driven by data. In the words of Lambert and colleagues in this book, they cannot be directed. Linear top-down leadership may work for a short time for simple outcomes, but more sophisticated learning needs to be accompanied by more sophisticated leadership.

Surprisingly, many kinds of leadership do not have that necessary consistency between how leadership is carried out and what it is that is being led. Distributed leadership can occur in Lesson Study and learning communities and also in sects and cults. Transformational leadership, as the authors point out, is often shared and dispersed, but in its origins, it was also, and still sometimes is, charismatically and emotionally manipulative.

There are exceptions. *Inclusive leadership* insists not only on inclusion of all students and their identities in a common learning process, but also inclusion of the adults in decisionmaking about those processes. *Sustainable leadership* supports educating students for sustainable development but also insists that these goals cannot and should not be conducted in schools that are organizationally unsustainable— where education for sustainable development programs are championed by a single leader, where there are no plans or processes for leadership succession, or where those programs are pursued in elite suburban schools while their impoverished neighbors are condemned to instruction only in standardized basics. *Uplifting leadership* asks us to uplift the people we serve, such as our students, by uplifting the people who serve them, especially their teachers. And Linda Lambert's own earlier work on *constructivist leadership* calls for thoughtful, problem-solving leaders who work collaboratively to develop thoughtful, problem-based learning processes.

While this book addresses the specific question of liberating leadership capacity, it depends even more centrally on the basic idea of liberating leadership. There are two senses to this core concept. First, education and learning must be about liberation of the human spirit, of the capacity to learn and inquire. It must release people from autocracy, repression and dependency. In the words of Eric Fromm, "creativity requires the courage to let go of certainties." Fromm was a celebrated mid-20th-century psychoanalyst and Jewish immigrant to the United States who argued for the importance of freedom in the face of authoritarianism and destructiveness. But his words were not meant to inspire the individualistic libertarianism of freedom from bad things. In his classic book, *Escape from Freedom*, Fromm described freedom as something that was rooted in the solidarity and spontaneity of human association and relationships, not in the escape from social interaction or regulation.

This is the second sense of liberating leadership described by Lambert and her colleagues in this book. Liberating leadership capacity is about liberating and releasing leadership capacity among others, not just by removing restrictions and letting things go but by taking deliberate actions, so that people learn to rid themselves of dependency on false certainties in favor of collective judgments developed with others. As the authors point out, developing people's capacity here does not just mean giving them training and resources; it means helping people to help themselves, just as it did when the concept was first articulated to describe supporting people in less-developed economies.

Liberating Leadership Capacity shows that the idea of liberation in leadership needs structure, protocols, and attention. It has to move through different stages, and leaders have to be attentive to which stage their community has reached so it can benefit most from the most appropriate kind of leadership. The book is grounded in the deepest, most democratic and humanistic philosophies that Lambert herself has exercised and promoted throughout most of her career. Here, she draws on the considerable work of her colleagues Diane Zimmerman and Mary Gardner to expand the reach of her ideas and the way they apply to schools in America and across the world.

Liberating leadership capacity is a commitment and a disposition. It is also a skill. As the authors of this book say, it is "the facilitation of constructivist approaches to visioning, discourse, inquiry, problem solving, reflection, and self-assessment" (p. 23) as collaborative processes.

There are many very good ideas in this book, and there is also great wisdom. It is a book that can not only set you and your school free but also set you off in a determined direction to foster a more inclusive and inspiring place for your students and fellow educators alike.

—Andy Hargreaves
Brennan Chair in Education
Boston College
February 2016

Preface

America's democratic education system has always had lofty goals: from the establishment of public schools to protect the common weal and foster informed citizenship, to John Dewey's belief that all children should realize their full potential, to a desire over the past few decades to make college a realistic goal for all students. Yet the current educational agenda seems to have veered off course. How is it that the educational focus has become so narrow that the emphasis is on micromanaging standards through benchmarking and assessment and not about developing intellect, social capacities, or curiosity? In the quest for accountability, have educators and families lost something? How is it that the wise counsel of Dewey and his promotion of education as a shared process of knowledge creation and meaning-making have been neglected?

Dewey's advocacy for connected knowing, which in this culture of measurement has been given little attention, ought not be forgotten and should inform current efforts to increase educational attainment. Shared meaning-making and knowledge creation are essential guiding principles that are critical for both learning and leadership, and they need to be reinserted into the reform equation. In 1995 Lambert coined the term *constructivist leadership*, and in the first book (Lambert et al., 1995) on this topic, the authors defined constructivist leadership as "the reciprocal processes that enable participants in an educational community to construct meanings that lead towards a common purpose of schooling" (p. 29).

In the second edition, the authors specifically stated, "The function of leadership must be to engage people in the processes that create the conditions for learning and form common ground about teaching and learning" (2002, p. 35). These authors now believe, more than ever, that to foster leadership capacity, the learning community and those who inhabit it need to be liberated from the tyranny of serial edicts. The responsibility for such liberation begins with policies that vest teachers as learning leaders. These leadership ideas were invested in the concept of "leadership capacity as broad-based, skillful participation in the work of leadership" (Lambert, 1998, 2003). Ultimately, the responsibility for the development of high leadership capacity lives within self-organizing leadership communities.

Throughout their careers as appointed leaders, the authors have come to trust the potential of collective wisdom to promote the common weal and create informed communities and a new citizenry—one that is self-motivated to organize for continuous learning. In the years since the first edition of *The Constructivist Leader*, much has happened relating to the national policy agenda: No Child Left Behind, Common Core State Standards (CCSS), Race to the Top, assessment variations (some performance oriented), and test scores tied to teacher evaluation.

Yet now there may be a new window on the future of education. On December 10, 2015, President Obama signed the bipartisan Every Student Succeeds Act (ESSA). This act dismantles the massive federal role in education, relocating the authority for reform to the states, intermediate units, districts, and communities. Gone is the national push for CCSS, adequate yearly progress (AYP), and required reporting of failing schools. While states must still create standards and administer tests in elementary and secondary school in order to receive Title I funds, the role of the federal government has been relegated to that of a more distant partner.

Every Student Succeeds is a response to the realization that, after decades of policies focused on top-down reforms, the United States still fell far short of its historical drive to achieve equity for all students and foster world-class achievement. Students and parents report that school is something that is done to them, not a place where they are challenged to think about and respond to the important issues of our time. Educators report being confined and guided by top-down reforms and managers. Will these perceptions change? Will the shifting of authority once again broaden inequality among regions of the country? Possibly. Yet the time is ripe for another way. If equity of opportunity and outcomes is still a major goal of educational reform, then the notion of sharing leadership for improved educational practice and the development of knowledge has never been more urgent.

Several themes weave and interconnect throughout this text: leadership capacity, the relationship between professional learning and design thinking, the reciprocal processes of leadership, the democratization of knowledge, adaptive policies, and systemic change. We have selected national and international programs that richly manifest these themes.

Chapters 1 and 2 of *Liberating Leadership Capacity: Pathways to Educational Wisdom* set the stage by tracing the movement toward more-democratic leadership approaches during the past quarter century and establishing an expanded conception of leadership. Constructivist leadership and leadership capacity are fully interconnected for the first time, as the aim of leading becomes fostering capacity through the complex, dynamic processes of purposeful, reciprocal learning.

New discoveries in complexity theory, ecology, and neuroscience situate constructivist learning and leading as an extension of what living systems naturally have been primed to do—adapt and learn. Citing extensive current research on learning and systems thinking, we breathe fresh air into the work of leadership while challenging reform dominions that have heretofore stifled creativity and innovation. Germane to this discussion is the theory of emergence in which many parts join together to create a coherent whole that is greater than the sum of the parts. Indeed, the reciprocal processes of liberated leadership capacity create the state of emergence in which groups and communities become wiser and clearer about their purpose, beliefs, and actions.

The success of future generations demands a leadership approach that focuses on capacity building and promotes resilient, adaptive learners, both students and adults. Leadership capacity that fosters broad-based, skillful participation in the work of leadership is essential if a new generation of thought leaders is to emerge. Liberating leadership capacity in organizations and individuals illuminates complex puzzles around shared dilemmas of practice and fosters a creative mindset for tackling even the most intractable problems. From such leadership the potential emerges for profound practices based on inquiry and evidence, discourse, reflection, and action.

Chapter 3 brings forth a fresh perspective on professional learning, with a focus on design thinking as a promising avenue for self-organizing learning experiences. When we explore the ways in which high leadership capacity cultures shape professionalism and enhance professional growth, new designs emerge. Professional learning brings renewal and motivates communities to focus on the development of deep, sustained knowledge across a career. When teachers collectively design learning with an eye to increasing collective knowledge, they speak with the voice of leadership.

Historically, terms like *accountability* and *fidelity* were simplified into archaic notions of followership; ideas of integrity and moral purpose were lost in the lack of deep thinking on the part of professionals. While most teachers irregularly participated in professional development workshops designed for them, few were immersed in a learning culture. Lost in adherence to compliance were notions of learning as a natural process, a creative process, initiated by learners and provoked by curiosity and unanswered questions. Attention needs to be paid to capacity building over the span of a career.

Chapter 4 identifies four dimensions of collaboration that increase both skill and participation—the essential elements of high capacity communities. These are the reciprocal processes of leadership. Darling-Hammond (2013) cites several large-scale studies that define "community building" as essential for deepening teacher knowledge and increasing achievement. She highlights the importance of sharing intellectual purpose and collective responsibility for student learning. Every professional needs to understand his or her contribution to a community of learners.

The authors' updated application of the pedagogy of constructivism promotes depth, complexity, and variety so that students and educators are successful members of a caring learning community—free to wonder about the world they live in, free to attribute meaning to experience. This critical act—the negotiation of meaning—reminds learners and leaders that the journey for wisdom is lifelong and is never achieved by the mandated, narrow reforms. When professionals understand how to make a difference, they contribute to a larger view of schooling—one in which everyone is a leader responsible for constructing the shared understandings that lead to excellence.

Chapter 5 addresses the need for the profession to redefine its relationship to knowledge by envisioning the construction, acquisition, and generation of knowledge as more democratic. The democratization of knowledge arises from collective, practice-based wisdom. Practice-based wisdom draws from the consilience of knowledge, identified herein as "knowledge fields." Knowledge, once narrowly defined and bounded, has grown exponentially through the unfolding of electronic media. As knowledge is opened to fresh democratic approaches, educational reformers also must liberate the professional voices of teachers and other educational partners who can define their own pedagogy. Such an expansive view of education, devoid of recipes and checklists, and characterized by complex and nuanced thought and action, is required. This democratization of knowledge finds strong grounding in educational research and practice, and has the potential for fostering commitment and passion in educators and the larger community.

Chapter 6 contends that change is a natural process, one derailed by linear, controlled, and narrowly focused attention to reform agendas. This chapter describes systemic change in the light of complexity theory and the reciprocal processes of leadership, thus questioning traditional, timeworn undertakings. Further, the authors assert that nested systems are fluidly interconnected and made functional through collaborative work and adaptive policies. Questions of sustainability call forth domestic and global programs characterized by lasting leadership capacity. The selected global programs suggest a promising consensus: national commitments to teacher professionalism and experiential curriculum as the foundations for systems change and 21st-century student learning.

The Epilogue calls forth the understandings herein and envisions wisdom as an emergent process. Further, the perception of human insignificance in the context of cosmic vastness is countered by the deep significance of full participation in the evolution of knowledge and life. The authors contend that constructivist leadership makes wise schools possible—school communities that gain insight into the challenges and possibilities of a shared future.

Liberating Leadership Capacity is designed for adult learners in all stages of life and in all roles created to guide the processes of educational improvement. These roles include students and instructors in colleges and universities; school, district, regional, state, national, and global educators; governmental policymakers and legislators; nongovernmental organizations and research foundations; and educational entrepreneurs. In this book's most intimate application, it is hoped that teachers will model and teach students to find their own leadership voices.

Acknowledgments

During the years since the conception of *The Constructivist Leader* (Lambert et al., 1995, 2002), *Who Will Save Our Schools: Teachers as Constructivist Leaders* (Lambert et al., 1997), *Building Leadership Capacity in Schools* (Lambert, 1998), and *Leadership Capacity for Lasting School Improvement* (Lambert, 2003), the authors of this book have had the privilege of working with and learning from numerous educators who have enriched the fields of learning and leadership. We are honored to acknowledge and include the research and practice of many of them in this book. They told us their stories and shared rich insights along the way. These contributors include Julie K. Biddle, professor and chair of initial licensure programs, School of Education, Antioch University, Ohio; Edward F. Burgess IX, associate executive director, San Juan Teachers Association, Sacramento, California; Gail Epps, program manager, new teacher induction, Montgomery County Public Schools, Maryland; Aaron Grossman, teacher on special assignment, Douglas County, Nevada; Linda Henke, director, Center for Transformational Leadership, Santa Fe, New Mexico; Jan Huls, former principal, Garfield School, San Leandro, California; Kathleen Huntington, teacher, The Athenian School, Danville, California; Ryan Land, manager, corporate affairs and organizational development, Manitoba Operations, Thompson, Manitoba; Marcie Logie, facilitator, Kent ISD Teacher Leadership Academy, Grand Rapids, Michigan; Pamelia Luttrull, principal, Lewis Elementary, Dallas, Texas; Nikki Rivera, director, Culture, Equity, and Leadership Team, Denver Public Schools, Colorado; Mark Silver, head of Hillbrook School, San Jose, California; April Smock, teacher, The Athenian School, Danville, California; Dale Skoreyko, principal of McNally High School, Calgary, Canada; Cathryn Smith, assistant professor, Brandon University, Manitoba, Canada; William Sommers, consultant, Austin, Texas; Jeffrey Stec, executive director, Citizens for Civic Renewal, Cincinnati, Ohio; Gail Taylor, founder and chair, Tomorrow Makers, Gualala, California; Betsy Warren, senior program consultant, New Teachers Project, Santa Cruz, California; and Wendy Westsmith, principal, Northside School, Black Oak Mine District, Georgetown, California. Thanks to Melissa Santos-Carthen for her excellent assistance with graphics.

Further, we thank three individuals who lent their experience and editing expertise to this book: Morgan D. Lambert, retired school district superintendent; Deborah Walker, president and CEO, Center for Teaching and Learning, Louisville, Kentucky; and Marty Krovetz, director, LEAD (an affiliated center of the Coalition of Essential Schools) and professor emeritus, educational leadership, San Jose State University, California. Both Morgan and Deborah were coauthors of *The Constructivist Leader* (1995, 2002).

We offer a special thank you to Jean Ward, consulting senior acquisitions editor, and John Bylander, production editor, both with Teachers College Press, who generously worked with us to bring *Liberating Leadership Capacity* to fruition.

LIBERATING
LEADERSHIP
CAPACITY

CHAPTER 1

Leadership Redesigned

Ask a thousand random individuals about one of the most persistent problems in schools, organizations, and countries today and you are likely to hear: leadership. Yet there is little understanding about this elusive concept. Many hold a belief that in times of distress people often look for someone to be in control, a directive leader who can tell them what to do. School boards seek out dominant superintendents who can "take charge"; schools are assigned principals to guide or push teachers into current reforms and fads. We challenge the contention that directive leadership is justified. Schools and organizations are rich with talented, thoughtful individuals who, when given the opportunity to work in open, engaging, and democratic cultures, consistently emerge as leaders and innovators. Adults learn; children learn. Creating these learning, leading schools and organizations is the mission of this book.

This chapter traces the transformative changes that have taken place in understandings of leadership during the past quarter century and offers a new definition of the concept. This provocative evolution has reframed the way leaders, leadership, and leadership capacity are defined—and therefore practiced—in leadership communities. How leadership is defined will determine how, when, and in what ways people participate. Leadership must offer a perspective designed to invite equitable participation, engage collaboration, and create sustainable organizations.

OAK VALLEY MIDDLE SCHOOL

Our story begins at Oak Valley Middle School at 4:00 P.M. on a Wednesday afternoon. (Oak Valley Middle School is a fictitious name. The stories about the school in this text are drawn from a composite of schools directly observed by the authors.) The school, built in the early 1970s, is situated in a low-income, moderately transient community on the outskirts of a major midwestern town. The culture of the school was not unlike many others: The principal led, faculty members were occasionally consulted but primarily worked alone, teachers did not perceive themselves as leaders, and mandated programs were administered by the district. Tensions arose over daily routines such as yard supervision and other extracurricular duties. Student performance and staff cohesion had been marginal until a new principal, a counselor, and two new teachers came to the school 3 years earlier. Now, this faculty is well steeped in norms of collaboration, dialogue, reflection, and inquiry. It is emboldened by a growing track record of successful cooperative action.

An English teacher, Joan, enters the library, early for the scheduled staff meeting, grabs a chair from one of the tables and sets it in the center of the room. Other teachers enter and follow her lead. Within a few minutes, 19 middle school teachers are formed into a circle. The principal has a critical time conflict and will be late.

"Just when I had the writing standards built into my curriculum, along comes a new list similar to the last, yet different. Much more complex. Listen to this. I am quoting from the Common Core State Standards information adopted by the district. 'Use narrative techniques, such as dialogue, pacing, description, and reflection to develop experiences, events, and/or characters.'" Joan pauses.

Isaac, the music teacher, responds empathically. "You're an experienced teacher, Joan. I haven't seen you thrown like this before. Is there more?" Others are silent. Waiting.

"Thanks, Isaac," says Joan. "It goes on, '. . . then pair it with all the standards on argumentative writing.' I hardly know where to start."

The math teacher chimes in: "We need to approach this as a team. The new Common Core has been adopted by the state. Correct?" The counselor nods.

"But there aren't history standards yet, just nonfiction reading and writing standards. And math," adds the veteran history teacher.

"No, no history standards yet. I think they're coming," says Wayne, a new core teacher. Others look at him expectantly. "We were working with these standards last year in my teacher certificate program. My observation is that they're a bit linear and avoid some crucial areas of learning, but there are ways to work with them—and benefit from them."

"I hope you're right. That's not how I see it right now. I'm weary from the cycle of new initiatives." Colleen, another English teacher, pauses, takes a deep breath. "I'm feeling successful right now with our literacy program. . . . I guess I don't want to upset the apple cart."

"Very understandable," says Aretha, the principal, as she enters the library, pulls up a chair, and joins the circle. "We share the familiar experience that imposed change can be frustrating," she says, speaking directly to Colleen. Scanning the room, she prompts, "Fill me in."

A veteran science teacher turns toward the principal. "We were discussing the new Common Core State Standards. So far we've heard several concerns: They are complex, linear, and may even discourage intellectual curiosity. They lack content in the social sciences and sciences. Wayne says they hold promise. But, as Colleen noted, we don't want them to dismantle successful practice."

Feeling heard, Colleen takes a deep breath and slides back into her chair.

"Thanks," says Aretha. "That's helpful. Sorry I'm late." She pauses and glances around the room.

"My sister teaches in Ohio," begins John, a second-year English teacher. "She hasn't been able to teach creative writing for more than a year. Just the essay."

A new science teacher, Raul, listens carefully, glancing around the room. "My primary concern is that the standards could crowd out and devalue student experiences and prior knowledge. We are working to incorporate how students learn—how we learn, for that matter. We all need to explore, to make sense of what we're learning. We have to leave space for connecting the curriculum, for asking questions."

"Well said, Raul. That's exactly our aim here: to incorporate how we know students learn," says Aretha. "District plans are under way to tackle this work as a cluster of schools working together."

The technology teacher, George, waits for a moment of silence, then begins. "I am very moved by Raul's and Aretha's comments. We have to ask hard questions about these standards. We also need to work with them. Working across schools can be very productive."

"As Isaac suggested earlier, we'll approach this dilemma as the team we've become," says Joan. "After all, we have the capacity to face this challenge," she observes, noticeably more relaxed. Several teachers and the principal nod.

"So let's come up with a plan, a plan to bring our experiences together in preparation for the cross-school meetings," suggests the art teacher.

The faculty at Oak Valley School designed a set of approaches for working within the CCSS that had been adopted by the district. Initially, these steps included reviewing the standards together, watching a video interview of the writers of the standards to understand their perspectives and expectations, and meeting in vertical teams (6th–8th grades) to explore cross-discipline impact.

Members of the Oak Valley staff were provoked into reflection and action by challenging external demands. What processes led to a collaborative plan for working within the standards? What actions will the staff take? What distinguishes this school event from a multitude of others? The quality of the staff members' thinking, their skills, and their relationships was different from that at many other schools. The faculty were willing to surface assumptions, critique the standards, and seek to understand each person's viewpoint; they were ready to inquire into practice by posing questions and designing research approaches. When tensions occurred, faculty members sought to acknowledge and clarify differing points of view. The principal was engaged but not the center of the process; each teacher took responsibility for participating in the collaboration. They were not powerless in the face of state policy, but were ready to take actionable steps, for they possessed a passion for discovery and a sense of collective agency.

Collective agency—the deep capacity to work together—had not always been the case at Oak Valley Middle School. Three years earlier, staff members began to reconceptualize leadership—how they could engage as co-leaders. By defining leadership broadly, they removed the concept from role and person and embedded it in the center of their collaborative community.

SHIFTS IN LEADERSHIP THINKING
CHANGE THE WORLD OF SCHOOLING

For the past 30 years, the authors of this book have worked in multiple leadership positions and participated in many forums designed to explicate essential leadership capabilities observed in successful schools like Oak Valley. Many writers and thinkers have struggled with what it means to be a good leader. An abundance of ideas sprang forth as state after state recognized the importance of leadership in schools and organizations, and grappled with their own training programs. A new wave of change was taking place. But where was it headed?

More than 25 years ago, Lambert was invited by Phil Schlechty to a conversation on leadership in Kentucky to define an "enlightened approach to leadership." The question was simple: What is good leadership? Brainstorming by educators from across the country began. "Leadership is: good communication, being trustworthy, respecting others, being decisive. . . ." Such attributes and traits flew onto the charts. The group gained momentum, demonstrating a shared assurance that they were in pursuit of those magical ingredients that make for "good leaders," "good leadership." Surely, one and the same.

This Kentucky experience was a moment of epiphany into a new future for leadership. Narrow views of leadership were vigorously questioned, noting that "leader" and "leadership" typically were not distinguished in the minds of those who wrote about and applied these concepts. Leaders considered "exceptional and skillful," virtually always individuals in formal positions of authority, were described as being vested with a set of leadership skills and personal traits that enabled them to make the school's important decisions and lead others in their implementation—to influence, pressure, and nudge toward school goals. After all, hadn't the great leaders of history—those whom history designated as having changed the direction of civilizations—possessed remarkable leadership attributes? Didn't these visionary characteristics entice and enchant followers?

During the past century, an array of writers and philosophers, including John Gardner, James MacGregor Burns, Warren Bennis, Peter Drucker, Michael Fullan, and Tom Sergiovanni, among others, described and reinforced the myth of the flawless single leader who is moral, courageous, bold, audacious, compassionate, and ethical. While these attributes are important, when they are assigned to a singular, designated leader with formal authority, the chances of others assuming leadership roles are diminished—one of the almost inevitable downfalls of charisma.

Traditional leadership models persist in many schools and celebrate the single enlightened leader. At the heart of many traditional views of leadership is the belief that there are only certain individuals who can lead.

Excessive centralization of authority, as applied in traditional leadership, constrains the maturation of a democratic citizenry, often seducing followers to believe that significant formal authority invested in the chosen leader can solve intractable problems. And what about the rest of us who have not been so anointed?

The uses of authority present a dangerous dilemma: a codependency, or dominance, sure to steer in unhelpful directions, away from a complex notion of leadership capable of more fully democratizing and building community capacities. Individuals, concepts, and institutions needed to be liberated from the hold placed on them by traditional notions of leadership and followership. As Uhl-Bien, Marion, and McKelvey (2007) claimed, "Leadership is too complex to be described as only the act of an individual or individuals; rather, it is a complex interplay of many interacting forces" (p. 314).

A QUARTER CENTURY OF LEADERSHIP EVOLUTION

By the early 1990s, researchers began to question the fundamental assumptions about who could lead and who could learn. Societies entered the knowledge era, no longer satisfied with the industrial era in which bureaucratic hierarchies managed workers and followers toward production. This knowledge era demanded that each person possess greater knowledge and expertise (McKelvey, 2001); a sense of agency and commitment were vital. Writing from a biological perspective, King, Johnson, and Van Vugt (2009) pointed out that the history of human and other animal dominance that originally formed the basis of leadership was no longer suited for complex, knowledge societies.

The knowledge era drew from the sciences as well. In 1992, Wheatley composed the first edition of *Leadership and the New Sciences*, noting the parallels between the fluidity and unpredictability signaled by quantum physics, chaos theory, and the world of leadership. She noted that individuals created information in interaction with one another, and information spiraled into new meanings. The observation that the new sciences are integral to the understanding of leadership is also supported by research on the brain.

New understandings of the brain confirmed that learning could be understood as a constructivist process through which the learner imbued new ideas and experiences with meaning. The brain was a malleable, rather than a fixed, organ and learning could be undertaken at any age. As the brain grew, it formed relational maps, neural networks, creating an ever-more-complex organ capable of accessing new knowledge and engaging in multi-layered relationships.

Layered relationships and networked interactions provided the underlying framework for sharing leadership fundamental to democracy. Mary Parker Follett (1924), a pioneer in the field of organizational theory and behavior, insisted that a person should look beyond the appointed leader for guidance. Kocolowski (2010) summed up nearly 8 decades of organizational thinking in his observation: "Shared leadership is a relational, collaborative leadership process or phenomenon involving teams or groups that mutually influence one another and collectively share duties and responsibilities" (p. 24).

With the writing of *The Constructivist Leader* (Lambert et al., 1995, 2002), the authors presented concepts that promised another seismic shift in the leadership landscape. *Leader* and *leadership* were not used interchangeably, since leadership could be understood as an integral part of a larger ecology, not as an individual. Complex ecological systems recognized that interaction and interdependence among individuals created unique learning environments greater than the sum of their parts. Therefore, considering the two terms, *leader* and *leadership*, as interchangeable narrowed and limited the scope and dynamics of leadership.

Drawing from decades of observations and studies of the nature of leadership and learning, the authors of that text proposed a new idea: "leadership as reciprocal, purposeful learning and action in community" (Lambert et al., 1995, p. 29). Authority, expectations, and knowledge would no longer be vested in only a few formal leaders and their followers.

Constructivist leadership challenged traditional thinking regarding the concept of leadership. At that time, the gap between traditional leadership and this newer conception was dichotomized (see Figure 1.1). The movement from traditional to constructivist leadership shifted from top-down, directive leadership to horizontal, shared leadership.

Figure 1.1. A Comparison of Traditional and Constructivist Leadership

Traditional Leadership: Approaches and Action	Constructivist Leadership: Approaches and Action
Formal leader's vision	Shared vision
Single/few leaders with formal authority	Multiple leaders including all who have a vested interest
Leader may or may not ask for advice, recommendations, and input	Full participant engagement in design, action, outcomes, and responsibility
Leader controls information, goals, action, policy	Participants involved in dialogue to understand information and determine goals, actions, policy
Data selected and delivered top-down to participants as information and used to evaluate success and judge effectiveness	Inquiry into effectiveness involves all participants and data Multiple measures of performance used to assess progress
Tasks are distributed and delegated by formal leader	Participants have fluid roles based on expertise, shared responsibility
Implementation committees or assigned departments	Skilled, diverse teams with facilitators, dialogue, inquiry, action
Staff training, technical coaching	Professional learning, cognitive coaching, learning communities, dialogue, and inquiry
Employees report problems, expecting leader to solve them	All participants discuss and solve problems
Entrepreneurship limited to a few and is proprietary	Entrepreneurship encouraged as a generative, innovative practice and shared with interested groups

On the eve of the publication of the first edition of *The Constructivist Leader*, ideas about the nature of leadership were beginning to come from multiple sources. Ronald Heifetz (1994) declared *adaptive leadership* to be a problem-solving process, a set of strategies and practices that helped organizations break through gridlocks, accomplish deep change, and develop the adaptability to thrive in competitive and challenging environments. Such leadership could be practiced by anyone in the organization. Heifetz also commended the parallel notion of *generative leadership*, defined broadly as leadership fostering innovation, adaptation, and high performance over time.

Fritjof Capra (personal communication, September 1996–April 1997); Spillane, Halverson, and Diamond (2004); Andy Hargreaves (2005); and Brent Davies (2005) began to view leadership as "processes among individuals," which suggested relationships, rather than the journey of the lone individual. Beginning in 1999, Spillane's work in *distributed leadership* held many parallels to the emerging concepts of leadership. Certainly the notion of stretching leadership across participants, sharing in the conversations and decisions together, was immediately appealing. Distributed leadership was evolving into leadership practice rather than being seen as a leader and his or her roles or functions. Spillane, Camburn, Pustejovsky, Pareja, and Lewis (2006) declared that "leadership activity is constituted—defined or constructed—in the interaction of leaders, followers, and their situation in the execution of particular leadership tasks" (p. 33). Including "followers" in this statement strikes at the heart of the difference between constructivist and distributed approaches—equitable interactions capable of creating and responding to complex systems versus the leader–follower dichotomy. In 2009, however, Harris no longer used *followers* in her own description of distributed leadership; indeed, she cited from Bennett, Wise, Woods, and Harvey (2003): "seeing leadership as the outcome of the dynamics of interpersonal relationships (an emergent property of the group) rather than just individual action" (p. 6).

By the late 1990s, in the health field, *complexity leadership theory* (Marion, 1999) began to emerge as integrating complex adaptive systems and leadership into a solid theory compatible with constructivist leadership. Uhl-Bien et al. (2007) offered, "Complex Leadership Theory is a framework for leadership that enables the learning, creative, and adaptive capacity of complex adaptive systems in knowledge-producing organizations" (p. 304). This theory involved three dimensions of leadership: adaptive, enabling, and administrative. The adaptive dimension signals a process, not a person or role; the enabling dimension creates the conditions for emergence of innovation. However, the administrative dimension adheres to trait theory in that individuals in roles of authority attend to the bureaucratic functions of the organization.

Imagine a school in which adults engage in rich conversations, such as Oak Valley Middle School, cited above. These conversations are networks of interactions in which individuals evolve in their thinking and knowledge and the group emerges into a new place of understanding. Each person and the group change as they create understandings that could not have been discovered by any one person alone. This is what is called a dynamic network, in which each person is altered and the group as a whole adapts and self-organizes. When a teacher at Oak Valley says, "Let's choose one standard, teach it across the curriculum, and evaluate its outcomes," the process of self-organization is under way.

A new century was upon us. From all corners of the English-speaking world, perceptions of leadership began to converge.

A NEW CENTURY OF LEADERSHIP DAWNS

In 2005, British educator Brent Davies launched an effort to explicate and define the several forms of leadership on the world stage. Davies captured and sought to integrate the essentials of leadership, with the exception of complexity leadership theory, in this seminal text. Thus, by the first decade of the new millennium, the broad range of leadership paradigms gave voice to individuals within organizations, broadened the field of interactions, and recognized essential leadership capacities. Numerous contributions were closely related.

Leithwood and Jantzi (2005) argued persuasively that the historic concept of *transformational leadership*, originated by James MacGregor Burns in 1978, had been the focus of rigorous research in recent years and now recognized these key characteristics: Transformational leadership is not about the behaviors (traits) of a charismatic individual but about the practices that are distributed collaboratively among staff members, and relationships are interdependent and involve parents and community members as well as professional staff. The idea that leadership emanates from a single leader has receded as a dominant concept. Rather, leadership is evolving into an interdependence of relationships.

It is notable that, of the other leadership paradigms included by Davies in 2005 in the classic *The Essentials of School Leadership*, none advocates command and control approaches to leadership. With the new millennium, leadership was being liberated from the bondage of traditional leadership. In the capstone of *The Essentials*, Andy Hargreaves (2005) describes leadership "as a process and a system, not as a set of personal, trainable and generic competencies and capacities that are possessed by individuals . . . as a process that influences and develops things that matter in ways that spread and last for the benefit of all" (p. 173). These remarkable changes in understandings of leadership were growing in abundance in the literature. However, the reality in schools still presented quite a different picture. In the United States, especially in low-performing schools, the mandate to produce higher test scores resulted in leader-centric change efforts such as stipulated minutes of instruction, pacing guides paired with benchmark assessments, and teacher evaluation tied to standardized test scores.

Within the same rich milieu of changing perceptions described by Hargreaves, more-focused research on women in leadership challenged the heavily male-dominated field of leadership (Lambert & Gardner, 2009). At first, cases were made that having more women in top leadership positions was the right thing to do. But as research findings were revealed, it became apparent that organizations with more women at the top were more successful. In other words, as Sheryl Sandberg (2015), author of *Lean In,* aptly writes, men are better off when more women are around because organizations in which more women participate evidence higher levels of success. Women are quicker to show empathy and caring (Brizendine, 2006) and more skilled in cooperation and collaboration—the essential skills of the new millennium.

In 2009, with the publication of "Leadership: Current Theories, Research, and Future Directions," Avolio, Walumbwa, and Weber undertook a comprehensive review of the literature. Most of the studies cited measured themselves against transformational leadership, considering it the major canon of leadership literature and practice. Strikingly, their summary conclusions do not differ significantly from those of Davies, above. Several conclusions claim that the direction of leadership for the previous decade involved (1) evolution into more holistic views, including complex and emergent dynamics in organizations; (2) attention to the linkage between leadership and outcomes; and (3) more leadership being distributed and shared in organizations. As will be noted below, the notion of "followership" was still persistent.

Figure 1.2 displays the evolution of leadership concepts during the past quarter century. The dimensions include (1) definitions of leadership involving trait theory and/or social dynamics; (2) who can lead; (3) the extent of "teamness" or collaboration; (4) relationships to complex dynamics, including self-organization and emergence, and (5) expected outcomes.

Note that while the traditional leadership concept is considered the most archaic and constricting and has been found to be ineffective, especially in bringing about sustainable change, it is very much alive in American and many international schools. A directive superintendent or principal is hired to implement a factory model of scripted instruction and test-based evaluation and curriculum. Each of the other approaches is evolving into a more sophisticated conception of social dynamics, often considering issues of emergence and co-construction. Therefore, each could be considered in flux, in process, including constructivist leadership.

So, how does our conception of leadership blend, complement, and differ from the roiling field of leadership development during the past quarter century—the decades since the publication of *The Constructivist Leader*?

Expanding Constructivist Leadership

While standing on the shoulders of our original concept of leadership and the rich ideas described above, constructivist leadership combines, expands, and adds multiple dimensions. We now define constructivist leadership as *fostering capacity through the complex, dynamic processes of purposeful, reciprocal learning*. This definition is instilled with the following characteristics of leadership vital to ushering the concept into new realms:

- Complex, dynamic processes, drawn from physics and biology, enable order to *emerge* from the interactions and interrelationships of multiple individuals and groups working in concert.
- Learning is, by its very nature, constructivist. Generative learning designs for children and adults need to regard constructivism as a fundamental framework.
- The concept of "follower" arrests the human brain in an old paradigm of inequities and subservience. "Participant" honors reciprocal, equitable relationships essential to democratization. Such relationships are critical in complex dynamic systems.
- Leadership capacity is the organizational presence of constructivist leadership. As a function of the breadth of participation and depth of skillful leadership actions, high leadership capacity creates the context in which successful, sustainable organizations emerge.
- By liberating leadership capacity, it becomes possible to democratize schools and organizations in local, regional, and global arenas.

Complex, Dynamic Systems. These systems are most evident in the human brain and nature—and in democratic environments. These complex processes are essential to the emergence of higher-order systems. Such systems thrive on diversity, the interplay of ideas, persons, and practices. Leadership is a form of learning, and both are complex, dynamic systems giving rise to the emergence of successful, sustainable schools and communities. By "emergence" we mean the development of patterns, characteristics, or capabilities (such as self-organization) arising through the interactions of individuals who, alone, do not possess those qualities. Such systems prompt outcomes and policies that are fluid, changing, and adaptive.

A prime barrier to such systems lies in separation of people, places, and spaces. Separation into classrooms, schools, departments, and other "silos," as well as isolation wrought by vast geographical terrains, inhibits essential interactions. Isolation from diversity—homogeneous schools, organizations, and communities—is among the most problematic conditions of all. Therefore, such systems must be artfully redesigned through connection, communication, and collaborative learning designs.

Senge, Scharmer, Jaworski, and Flowers (2004) claim: "Connectedness is the defining feature of the new worldview—connectedness as an organizing principle of the universe" (p. 188). Connectedness is essential to the creation of complex adaptive systems. Nearly a decade later, Alper, Williams, and Hyerle (2012) continued the crucial observations about connectedness: "To connect is one of our most fundamental human impulses—not just with others on a personal level, but with ideas as well. We are, as many brain researchers have noted, pattern seekers and meaning makers. To be human

Figure 1.2. Evolutionary Dimensions of Leadership

Leadership Models	Leadership Defined	Proponents
Traditional Leadership	• A leader with formal authority; directive, efficiency-based traits • Information/policies top down, centralized • Roles narrowly delineated, decontextualized • Uniform, predetermined outcomes (see Figure 6.1)	Taylor, Schenk, Bobbitt, Gulick, Urwick
Shared Leadership	• Leader traits humanistic, collaborative, empathic • Collaborative problem solving, culture • Leader roles shared among team members • Relationships important to organizational effectiveness • Expected to achieve shared goals	Follett, Gibbs, Barth, Sergiovanni, Conger, Westsmith
Transformational Leadership	• Leaders lead, followers follow • Aims to transform systems and individuals within systems • Interdependent, collaborative cultures • Leadership roles are shared among team members • Expected to achieve shared vision and goals	Burns, Leithwood, Kellerman, Henke, Avolio, Walumbwa, Weber
Adaptive Leadership	• Leadership as problem solving rather than trait theory • Can be practiced by anyone • Adaptiveness of highest importance • Outcomes: Problem solutions adapted to environment demands	Heifetz, Linsky, Grashow, Laurie, Argyris, Gardner, Kegan, Garmston

Leadership Models	Leadership Defined	Proponents
Constructivist Leadership I	• Redefined leadership as separate from trait theory and individual roles • Leadership as a form of reciprocal, purposeful learning • Participantship replaced followership; all can lead • Ecological context for the practice of leadership • Broad range of possible, unpredictable outcomes informed by shared vision	Lambert, Wheatley, Capra, Kegan, Costa, Walker, Senge, Davies
Distributed Leadership	• Trait theory premise, leader–follower dichotomy • Shared, distributed roles and authority • Leadership constituted in interactions among group members • Expected outcomes: Collaborative teams determine outcomes in concert with vision and goals	Spillane, Harris, Drucker, Burgess, DuFour, Murphy, Covey, Wenger, Lave
Complexity Leadership Theory	• Leadership context based on complexity theory, emergence of innovation and knowledge • Three leadership dimensions: adaptive, enabling, administrative • Maintains traditional, trait-based leadership roles for bureaucratic functions • Outcomes innovative, yet focused by administration	Uhl-Bien, Marion, Hazy, McKelvery, Schwandt, Lichtenstein, Adhadeff-Jones, Van Velsor
Constructivist Leadership II	• Leadership defined as fostering capacity through the complex, dynamic processes of purposeful, reciprocal learning • Complexity theory gives rise to self-organization and emergence • Reciprocal, purposeful learning is constructivist • Participantship rather than leader–follower • Leadership capacity as broad-based, skillful participation in the work of leadership • Expected outcomes: democratization	Lambert, Greene, Hargreaves, Fink, Southworth, Gardner, Zimmerman

is to be connected to others, to be engaged with others" (p. 14). In other words, relationships are the *synapses* of connectedness and the essence of complex systems. The systems to which we refer are constructivist.

Constructivist Learning. Such learning means the construction of meanings based on values, knowledge, and previous experiences. Each individual's perception of reality is unique, as is the meaning she or he assigns to ideas and experiences. These perceptions, although unique, become a tapestry of meaning making, creating, and knowing within a collaborative community. Such learning is generative; that is, the process of constructivist learning generates new insights, understandings, and concepts, thus altering the mind of the learner. The constructivist aspect of leadership involves these key elements: (1) *purpose*, (2) *reciprocity*, (3) *learning*, and (4) *community*. Such leading and learning experiences often entail the following:

1. *Evoking* our beliefs, assumptions, and perceptions. This can be facilitated through inquiry, narrative, reflection, and dialogue.
2. *Inquiring* into practice in order to discover new information and data. Questions, observations, action research, examining student work, and reading about best practices contribute to inquiry.
3. *Constructing* meaning or making sense of the discrepancies or tensions between what we believe and think and the new information we have discovered is essential. Such inquiry can reveal patterns from which inferences are made and tested as part of ongoing learning, thus contributing to a shared knowledge base.
4. *Acting collectively in community* comes as a result of learning and deciding together about what will be planned, created, or done differently. (Lambert, 2005, p. 96)

When *communities* become true learning communities, the group identity shifts toward a shared vision of purpose and value. Values cannot be coaxed or forced, but must be developed by conscious attention to reciprocal relationships and purpose. To be purposefully engaged in the world is a moral undertaking, meaning that values such as equity, democracy, human rights, caring, and social justice drive our behaviors. To act from this perspective takes courage, which comes more readily when the action is undertaken with others.

Members of the most successful learning communities consistently find themselves in a place similar to Oak Valley Middle School, where the work of leadership is to weave together meanings and experiences in relationship with others, igniting emergent outcomes. At this school, all involved revealed a form of leadership both reciprocal and purposeful. A cross-discipline integration of key Common Core State Standards emerged from the processes. Staff members understood the need to adapt standards to their own practice and values in order to make sense of what the standards could mean for themselves and students. When educators understand that they are largely in charge of their own learning and leading, they report having more ownership of and passion toward the work of teaching. They also report that it is hard work, but worth it.

Participantship. Participantship signifies a flatter organization, more equitable relationships, and mutual regard. Those who still grapple with followership are stuck in ancient terrains in which leaders occupied a narrow passage where there was room for only a few to guide, to pass. That narrowness etched in power and authority requires others to walk behind, being alert to cues from the "leader." "Followers" create hierarchy and nonequitable relationships that prevent complex systems from working. Followership continues to limit the definition of leadership and hence the capacity for self-determination.

In 2000, James MacGregor Burns was still grappling with the notion of followers that he had adhered to in the establishment of transformational leadership in 1978. He puzzled, "For me, nothing is more perplexing in the study of leadership than the role of followership. It would seem so simple on first glance—that leaders lead, and followers follow. But we know it is more complicated than that" (p. 11). Indeed it is.

In *Followership* (2008) and *The End of Leadership* (2012), Kellerman has sought to expand the concept of followership by giving it equal weight with the importance of leadership and context, speaking of the ground-up influence and demands of followers as consumers, Internet communicators, and revolutionaries. Why not relinquish the word *followership*? Leadership must honor the reciprocal, equitable relationships essential to democratization. Such relationships are critical in complex dynamic systems. Established authority cannot mandate this fluidity of leadership; it emerges out of the tasks, expertise, and needs of the community. There are successful schools and organizations where expertise, for instance, determines the leader. For example, when teachers define a focus such as problem-based learning, everyone may be invited to investigate the concept. As teachers gain new knowledge, they take the lead on school implementation. These are not followers, but leaders and participants.

Power has been a fundamental leverage in the leader–follower dichotomy. Without reciprocity, the balance of power is inevitably tilted. Reciprocity means we share mutual responsibility for one another's learning, as well as the learning of the community. It enables the pursuit of learning and leading within patterns of equitable relationships in which individuals are mutually committed and supportive of one another, rather than playing dominant or submissive roles. This central tenet requires learning from one another. Power that is horizontal and reciprocal is an empowering, essential aspect in the pursuit of collective agency.

Authority and power often go hand in hand. Power resides in each of us, and is actualized or more fully expressed when the culture is liberating and democratic, or harmfully focused when the culture is closed and authoritarian. In powerful organizations, reciprocal relationships encourage each to speak and contribute with an authentic voice—what is really meant, not what others might want to hear. Appointed authority, although important, privileges one voice over others. Unappointed or informal authority often is expressed by teacher leaders who influence one another through their knowledge, expertise, skills, and passion. At Oak Valley Middle, the teachers realized that Raul had recent experience from his graduate studies of the CCSS, which gave him informal authority.

Informal authority is the most desired exercise of authority in a democratic community because it is relational; relationships flatten hierarchies. Skill in influencing through informal authority—participation—is an important focus in successful leadership preparation programs focused on evoking group potential and bringing out the best in all participants (Garmston, 2012; Garmston & Zimmerman, 2013b). When these voices are heard within an open, stimulating environment, leadership responsibility expands, bringing more and more voices into the knowledge network.

When coauthor Mary Gardner became the superintendent of the Saratoga School District in California, she invited Linda Lambert and Emily Brizendine to study her practice. "What do you want to change in the culture of the school district?" Lambert and Brizendine asked. Gardner replied, "I want to create equitable power arrangements in the district, for educators to see one another as resources and not look to the superintendent as the sole resource." When asked, "How might we observe those changes?" she said, "Observe how teachers relate to the superintendent and one another in districtwide curriculum meetings." The data revealed that it took most of the year for teachers to stop turning toward the superintendent when a tough question was asked in order to discover the "right" or "approved" answer. Relationships and the culture reformed together.

Leadership Capacity. Both leadership and capacity are deepened by the expanded understandings of constructivist leadership. The work of such leadership aims for actions that create and utilize complex dynamic systems to build capacity in organizations. The concept of "capacity" as used in this text is drawn from international capacity-building programs designed to help people solve their own problems (Lambert, 1998, 2003). Capacity herein refers to an organization's capacity to work in concert to solve the most challenging problems of schooling. Such organizations unleash innate, often latent, leadership capacities in every individual.

Leadership capacity is defined as *broad-based, skillful participation in the work of leadership*. Understandings of skill, participation, and leadership encompass learnings from domestic and global settings as well. With the evolution of leadership, complexity theory, systems change, and sustainability, the concept of leadership capacity has expanded.

Democratization. Democracies require lateral interconnections among participants, for democracy is an emergent property that grows from these interactions and is made manifest through multiple structures. In global societies, this means certain rights or freedoms: of speech, religion, and the press; rule of law; civil and economic liberties. In a school, educators seek to establish values and purpose, working agreements, collaborative teams, learning designs and protocols. Further, democratization demands a global and authentic curriculum and learning that acknowledges the need for discretion, choice, creativity, and critical thought. These parallel constructs—in schools and societies—give rise to democracies.

When humans experience liberating, democratic, engaging cultures, the quality of thinking and action foreshadows and enables emergent, self-organizing conditions. This may be the most powerful and revolutionary statement made about prospects for societal and organizational improvement. Recently, Pentland (2014), writing in *Social Physics*, stated it well:

> Engagement—repeated cooperative interactions—builds trust and increases the value of the relationship, which lays the groundwork for the social pressure needed to establish cooperative behaviors. In other words, engagement builds culture. (p. 74)

An engaging, healthy democratic community creates something greater than the sum of its parts; information flows from the bottom up as well as laterally among participants, and the diversity of opinions offers new ways to think and behave. When groups self-organize, they *initiate* actions that promise to improve lives in schools and organizations and countries. Within a framework of democratic principles and structures, communities consistently find coherence, a unity leading in flexible, purposeful directions.

Constructivist leadership, then, is defined as *fostering capacity through the complex, dynamic processes of purposeful, reciprocal learning*. How leadership is defined makes all the difference in how people participate—in how participants show up to contribute as leaders, not followers. The leadership assumptions in Figure 1.3 might still be considered bold and audacious. Consider the expectation that "everyone has the right, the ability, and the responsibility to lead." This is in direct contrast to the codependencies formed under authoritarian leadership.

Figure 1.3. Constructivist Leadership Assumptions

1. Leadership is not trait theory; leadership and leader are not the same. Leadership emerges within community.
2. Everyone has the right, the ability, and the responsibility to lead. Initiating and self-responsible behaviors can create collaborative approaches that allow the group to self-organize, thus freeing groups from the dependency on authority.
3. Leadership is a shared endeavor, the foundation for the democratization of schools and organizations. Leading toward purposeful change is most effectively done in community.
4. Leadership requires the redistribution of power and authority; reciprocity is an essential condition of these complex adaptive processes.

Equipped with these assumptions and years of experience and research in schools, districts, and international organizations, the authors draw the distinctions further characterizing liberating leadership capacity. Shifting from the direction of a few to the participation of many enables shared vision, authority, dialogue, inquiry, problem solving, and innovation to emerge. Schools and organizations possessing these characteristics possess high leadership capacity. Oak Valley Middle School is in the process of becoming such a school.

This past quarter century—since the early 1990s—has seen a convergence of significant interwoven and parallel trends that unite to form the demand for even newer ways of thinking about leadership. They include (1) global shifts into knowledge-based, technological societies; (2) theories from physics and biology surfacing in the social sciences; (3) breakthroughs in neuroscience; (4) research on women's leadership; and (5) stunning failures in traditional leadership. These converging threads framed the burning question: "Isn't there a better way?" New insights into leadership have drawn the strings together and emerged with deeper understandings of how leadership manifests itself in organizations and broader communities.

Acts of Liberated Leadership

The call to leadership by committing to shared interactions within groups embedded in complex adaptive systems has never been stronger. The breadth of essential interactions is even more evident when considering the connections or learning processes among individuals in a school community. Leaders perform *acts of leadership* that foster learning together so a community can make decisions and create actions that grow out of the real dilemmas of teaching and learning—rather than engage in knee-jerk reactions to external demands such as those created by test scores and policy directives. A compelling question here is: How do leaders influence the behaviors of the entire community so the system will learn, adapt, and evolve in concert?

For those who do not find the separation of "leadership" from "leader" appealing, consider *acts of leadership*—that is, what leaders need to know and be able to do in order to exert such influence. Leadership capacity is liberated through both a redefinition of the concept of leadership and emergent leadership actions, thereby labeling the participatory actions taken by individuals as acts of leadership. Such acts ground practice in the specific behaviors, actions, and outcomes of individuals and groups exercising leadership. This applies to all participants in communities, especially teacher leaders.

The power of liberated leadership capacity present in small actions was revealed in yet another simple epiphany following a presentation for nearly 1,200 educators in Calgary, Canada, in 2003. It was the practice at the end of a session to ask for participant response. A young kindergarten teacher walked to the podium and said: "As I listened, I realized that *listening* is an act of leadership." She continued, "When I am respectfully listened to, I clarify my own ideas and strengthen my relationship with my listener." This teacher's comment encapsulated a concise summary of all that had been said about reciprocity, relationships, learning, and leadership. The young woman had assigned meaning to these ideas, making them her own.

In the following chapters, acts of leadership are described in detail. These acts, joined with a deep understanding of the assumptions and principles underlying leadership, enable educators to foster and liberate leadership capacity.

CONCLUSION

In Chapter 2, the unique meaning of leadership capacity is further explored. Starting with the tenets of constructivism, there is now a much larger question: How do we build the capacities of school cultures so educators can recapture the profession and become actionable leaders? Concurrently, how do we redesign schools and organizations to serve as the context for liberating leadership capacity?

The chapters in this book build on one another, weaving a spiraling tapestry. Chapter 2 discusses leadership capacity in depth. Chapter 3 provides a multifaceted understanding of adult and organizational learning within complex systems; Chapter 4 describes the dimensions of collaboration fostering leadership capacity in groups. Chapter 5 peers more deeply into collective knowledge creation. In Chapter 6, systems change sets the stage for global programs that emerge into democratic understandings and actions. In the Epilogue, the road to wisdom emerges from the ideas on liberating leadership capacity. The journey ahead is informed and influenced by bold expectations of leadership described in these chapters, thus liberating leadership from some of its historical moorings and the concomitant complexities.

QUESTIONS FOR REFLECTION

1. The text defines leadership as "fostering capacity in complex, dynamic processes enabling reciprocal, purposeful learning," a cultural rather than a traditional notion of leadership. How does this definition change the way you think about leading in your organization?
2. The evolution of leadership thought during the past quarter century could be considered remarkable. Consider the developments in leadership thinking summarized in Figure 1.2 and discuss which features are present in your school.
3. Figure 1.3 suggests assumptions underlying how leadership is manifested in a school. Do these assumptions differ from your own? Which assumptions would you want to examine more deeply? What would you add or change?
4. In preparation for Chapter 2, record the questions you have at this point. Begin to formulate your own theory of leadership capacity.

QUESTIONS FOR GROUP REFLECTION AND ACTIVITIES

1. The teachers, counselor, and principal at Oak Valley Middle School developed a plan to begin to integrate the Common Core State Standards into their practice. As one of the teacher leaders in this discussion, what question(s) might you pose to help the group clarify the road ahead?
2. Refer to Figure 1.1: Break into small groups to identify indicators that assess your school's leadership profile. Are your practices more in keeping with the right column or the left column—or somewhere in between? In the larger group, compare and contrast evidence with other teams. As differences of opinion arise, ask the group to summarize various viewpoints. Identify areas of common agreement and areas for growth.
3. Consider the Gardner story regarding equitable processes. Create four criteria your school could use to assess whether reciprocity is valued and practiced.

CHAPTER 2

Fostering Leadership Capacity

A deep concern for the achievement and sustainability of effective school reform led to a bridge from leadership into a broader arena: how systems or societies employ leadership to continually improve. The concept of leadership capacity grew from an interest in a set of understandings and processes promising to make the best of leadership thinking fully operational. The resulting framework was designed to enable the emergence of leadership capacity. Such emergence springs from simple interactions multiplied into large-scale change and involves shared goals, collaborative inquiry, dialogue, reflection, and collective action. These elements contribute to the establishment of a leadership culture or community.

The term *capacity*, when used as a social dynamic, is drawn from a long tradition of capacity building, especially in international settings. As noted in Chapter 1, capacity building enables a group of people to engage in and solve their own problems—rather than wait to be rescued, as many who were colonized came to expect; and to endure chaotic and difficult conditions in the interim. In the international arena, many of these undertakings related to access to natural resources, such as water, and to health concerns, such as hygiene, as well as to earning even a subsistence living. Schools and other social organizations are in need of similar problem-solving approaches, although the aims vary.

In schools, as in many other organizations, there often exist subtle barriers to problem solving, such as hidden assumptions and perceptions formed through experiences in closed systems. Declining enrollment and funding, a lack of informed leadership, and restrictive policies can add to the morass and make capacity building additionally complicated. Internal experiences of leadership, professional relationships, and collective knowledge can move educators forward in the journey toward school improvement.

Further, a school community often is confronted with unsatisfactory student performance, limited parent engagement, or poorly organized professional development. In order to address such barriers, groups or organizations share the need to build a sense of collective agency among their members. In education, as elsewhere, capacity building has been stalled by the dearth of discretion and choice at the local levels, and by stringent policies that rob educators of creativity and hamper innovation and commitment. Actively seeking capacity requires discretion and adaptive policies at the local level, "policies that can anticipate and respond to an array of conditions that lie ahead and can navigate towards successful outcomes when surprised by the unforeseen" (Swanson et al., 2009, p. 12).

Adding the term *leadership* to capacity changes the meaning of both by suggesting that capacity building is a function of leadership. To lead is to foster capacity in complex, dynamic systems through purposeful, reciprocal learning. This leadership perspective frames participation as essential to a democratic milieu. Broad-based participation can fully engage all in capacity building, while being ever conscious of the potential and meaning of dynamic interactions. This is what is meant by broad-based participation in the work of leadership.

Yet, participation in and of itself is not adequate, because—unless it is skillful—it can be chaotic and result in fragmented communities. As suggested above, it is *how* we participate, not just that we do. From these observations and understandings grew the full definition of leadership capacity as "broad-based, skillful participation in the work of leadership" (Lambert, 1998, 2003). Figure 2.1 shows a leadership capacity matrix in which each quadrant is considered an "archetype," meaning that with a certain degree of participation and skillfulness, there is a *tendency* to exist or form into a particular organizational profile. This tendency allows for the detection and expression of archetypal patterns, patterns that become more predictable when the context is deliberately designed. The contexts range from low to high states of leadership capacity.

LEADERSHIP CAPACITY AS AN ORGANIZATIONAL CONCEPT

Leadership capacity as an organizational concept frames the work of individuals within the system—influencing the patterns of relationships—and expands through the work. This concept arose from the repeated observation that all too often a school or district retreats into its former self when a dynamic principal or superintendent leaves. Yet social organizations do not "go home again"; indeed, this retreat finds a new nest—more cynical, dysfunctional, angry, and hopeless than where it began. Organizations may then take on substantial and costly reforms, only to be thrust into a shadow darker than before. Sustainability is an elusive yet essential quality in any reform effort and often is subverted by the loss of continuity and trust due to the early transfer of a superintendent, principal, or lead teacher (Fullan, 1998; Hargreaves, 2005; Lambert, 1998, 2003).

As noted above, leadership capacity requires an examination of interactions within the improvement domain: the breadth of participation and depth of skillfulness (understood as skills, understandings, and knowledge) in leadership. Participation as broad-based is closely related to many definitions and research analyses of "distributed leadership," in which leadership is envisioned as "stretched over" a large number of participants (Harris, 2008; Jones, Harvey, Lefoe, & Ryland, 2014; Spillane, 2002). Unfortunately, distributed leadership—a powerful concept—often is employed by superintendents and principals as a "delegation" model, which means handing out tasks while retaining the accompanying authority.

The skillful dimension of leadership capacity is not the delegation of work but rather the facilitation of constructivist approaches to visioning, discourse, inquiry, problem solving, reflection, and self-assessment among participants. These constitute many of the primary skills and knowledge that engage participants in the reciprocal learning processes of leadership. These are the interactions that create relational trust, thus spiraling the community into higher levels of capacity. Relational trust is characterized by openness, caring, and honesty, which promote vulnerability between and among others through influence and the sharing of information. This social glue is a critical key to school improvement and sustainability, and its erosion often impacts schools experiencing a change in funding or formal leaders. The cultivation of trust must not be considered a stand-alone skill. In a high capacity, high-performing school, relational trust must pervade all skills and dispositions of the leadership capacity matrix (Westsmith, personal communication, June 8–21, 2015).

Figure 2.1 is a matrix displaying four archetypes of school and organizational cultures in differing stages of leadership capacity development. The archetypes, which are discussed in detail below, are:

> *Archetype 1:* Low Leadership Capacity (Low Skillfulness/Low
>   Participation)
> *Archetype 2:* Fragmented Leadership Capacity (Low Skillfulness/High
>   Participation)
> *Archetype 3:* Limited Leadership Capacity (High Skillfulness/Low
>   Participation)
> *Archetype 4:* High Leadership Capacity (High Skillfulness/High
>   Participation)

Low Leadership Capacity Schools

Systems with low leadership capacity possess both low participation and low skillfulness in the work of leadership. That unfortunate dynamic or controlling condition can evoke overt defensive, protective human behaviors, such as lack of trust in the system's hierarchy, blaming, fear, codependency, and resistance to change. To sustain their own sense of professionalism, some

Figure 2.1. Leadership Capacity Matrix

<------------------- **Breadth of Participation** ------------------->

Low Capacity **Archetype 1**	**Archetype 2** **Fragmented Capacity**
• Principal as autocratic manager • Limited (one-way) flow of information; no shared vision • Codependent, paternal/maternal relationships; rigidly defined roles • Norms of compliance, blame, lack of trust; low sense of agency • Program coherence technical and superficial • Lack of innovation in teaching and learning • Student achievement is poor, or showing short-term, unsustainable improvements on standardized measures	• Principal as "laissez faire" manager; many teachers developing unrelated programs • Fragmentation and lack of coherence of information and programs; lack of shared purpose • Norms of individualism, lack of collective responsibility and agency • Undefined roles and responsibilities; situational trust • Spotty innovation with both excellent and poor classrooms • Student achievement appears static overall—unless data are disaggregated
Limited Capacity **Archetype 3**	**Archetype 4** **High Capacity**
• Principal and key teachers as purposeful leadership team • Limited uses of schoolwide data and information within leadership group • Polarized staff, pockets of strong resistance; limited trust outside team • Designated leaders act efficiently with a growing sense of agency; others serve in traditional roles • Reflection, innovation, and teaching excellence among selected teachers; program coherence still weak • Student performance static, or showing slight improvement	• Principals and teachers, as well as parents and students, as part of generative learning communities • Shared vision results in program coherence and collective agency • Inquiry leads to growth in knowledge and improved practice • Roles and actions reflect collaboration, trusting relationships, networking, and collective responsibility • Reflective practice consistently leads to innovation • Student performance, based on multiple measures, is steadily improving

(Vertical axis label, left side: ← Depth of Skillfulness ↑)

Adapted from Lambert (2003). © 2003 by ASCD (www.ascd.org). Reprinted with permission.

teachers retreat to classrooms and maintain effective teaching practices. The formal leader often manages staff through directive, autocratic management, with few invitations to share in decisions. Often school personnel passively wait for the next directive from the district, as well as the principal.

Student performance in low leadership capacity schools may experience a short upward spike with the introduction of scripted programs, but sustainably improving performance is rare or nonexistent. What often follows is another attempt to script and direct adult behaviors, further robbing professionals of opportunities to exercise autonomy and leadership. In a global society, the forceful removal of an autocratic leader tends to result in fragmented cultures that often lead to chaos and civil war (e.g., Afghanistan, Iraq, Egypt, Libya).

Fragmented Leadership Capacity Schools

These schools are characterized by high participation but low skillfulness and can result in school cultures with self-serving, independent actions without regard for the collective. Further, lack of experience and skill in responsible participation, such as adherence to agreed-upon working arrangements, sustained engagement, and open discourse, contributes to a "do your own thing" culture. Such a culture is what Fullan (1998) described as "balkanized" (p. 5). In a high school, for instance, eager, motivated students may be given preferential attention, while others "fall through the cracks." Fragmented leadership capacity schools are often designed to protect limited turfs—for example, resources being spent on athletic programs supported by enthusiastic and involved parents, or an outstanding drama or music program. Student leadership reflects the culture of the school and usually is drawn from those who are high performing academically and/or athletically. Students often form governments that focus on dances, team sports, rallies, and games, rather than evidencing concern for their less-involved peers. Many classrooms may be below par, with disengaged teachers who trust they will be left alone to do their own thing or who form small subcultures within the school.

Limited Leadership Capacity Schools

Conversely, limited leadership capacity schools exhibit low participation and higher skillfulness. Such leadership communities may involve a few able leaders who become increasingly stronger, finding interdependency among themselves. However, such bonds may not exist with many of the staff members. When school leadership fails, this cadre of leaders may wonder why they had difficulty engaging community members whom they expected to follow their lead. Teamwork may be limited to one leadership team, therefore not engendering the trust that emerges from shared work, and leaving relational trust uncultivated or underdeveloped.

Even though some classrooms in limited leadership capacity schools reveal excellent student performance, overall student achievement, as measured by test scores, may still appear static. As we have worked with numerous schools and districts, we find improving schools often get stuck in this place. Frustration among the few leaders runs high, causing team members to dwell on those who refuse to become engaged. So, how do such schools get unstuck?

High Leadership Capacity Schools

Ideally, the interaction of participation and skillfulness created through the work in leadership brings about dynamic, effective, and sustainable systems change in high leadership capacity schools and organizations. Teacher, as well as principal, student, and parent, leadership is central to broad-based collaborative participation. Successful systems—regularly involved in the reciprocal processes of leadership—possess vision-driven, inquiring, and self-organizing environments leading to democratic communities. In such co-constructed communities, a sense of social justice is pervasive—caring for the least privileged in society (Smith, 2014).

The expected outcomes of a high leadership capacity school culture are similar to those associated with the evolving concept of distributed leadership as described by the Royal Melbourne Institute of Technology (https://emedia.rmit.edu.au/distributedleadership). Jones et al. (2014) describe the heart of the concept: "Distributed leadership for learning and teaching is a leadership approach in which collaborative work is undertaken between (among) individuals who trust and respect each other's contributions" (p. 21). These authors note that this work involves reflective practice, planning and assessment, flexibility, shared engagement, and leadership capacity.

In recent years, distributed leadership—much like shared and transformational leadership—has taken on expanded meanings in different contexts. In *The Answer Is in the Room*, Blankstein (2011) argues that the fundamental question of school improvement and sustainability is the capacity to embed new practices as knowledge into the school culture. The focus, he suggests, "for developing leadership capacity and building the kind of community connected to a robust learning network of schools offers the best hope for sustained success" (p. 87).

Further, a fundamental outcome of the high leadership capacity school culture is the development of a sense of agency within and among staff members, and collective agency within the group. Rodney Ogawa (2005) refers to a sense of agency as the control one exercises over one's destiny and further analyzes the difficult struggle to develop and sustain agency within a deterministic, controlling environment. In a high leadership capacity school, conditions provide for discretion, choice, learning, and leading, and thus pave the way for agency. Agency must be collective as well as personal. This idea is fundamental to understanding leadership capacity.

David Brooks (2014) describes this internal capacity in the plight of author George Eliot's pursuit of agency as "the moment when she stopped being blown about by her voids and weaknesses and began to live according to her own inner criteria, gradually developing a passionate and steady capacity to initiate action and drive her own life." The development of one's own inner criteria—paired with the school's criteria for success—is basic to the emerging capacity of schools.

Bandura (1986, 2001) defines human agency within the construct of "self-efficacy"—a model of emergent, interactive agency. Self-efficacy describes the generative capability that mediates the relationship between knowledge and practice. While agency gives permission, efficacy focuses on how people judge or assess their own capabilities and ability to successfully act. This sense of efficacy directly relates to efforts put forth in the face of difficulties. As groups work together in successful learning and leadership communities, they develop collective efficacy, which endows them with a belief in their capacity to learn and lead—fundamental to the development of high leadership capacity schools.

IMAGES OF AUTHORITY DISTRIBUTION

Four images in Figure 2.2 capture the patterns of relationships and the movement from an authoritarian culture to a leadership culture that fosters capacity. A system such as that found in Image 4 is generative: That is, it generates ever higher, and more complex, levels of self-organization. Image 1 portrays the direction of power and authority experienced in a low leadership capacity school. Image 2 captures the disconnected distribution of singular work in a fragmented leadership capacity school. In Image 3, or limited leadership capacity, a small group of leaders attempts to shift to a horizontal distribution of authority in order to engage the whole community. This shift is yet to occur.

Image 4, the high leadership capacity school, describes the integrated system that is the goal of high leadership capacity organizations. Interactions among participants are moving in all directions, thus creating a resilient network of equitable leaders. It is from these reciprocal interactions that relational trust and sustainable improvements emerge. Even though a high leadership capacity school meets the requirements of sustainability, especially once self-organization is a routine occurrence, certain conditions and actions must be perpetuated in order to keep it from unraveling. This text is designed to describe how leadership capacity is liberated and how it is sustained.

Figure 2.2. Leadership Capacity Images: Authority Distribution

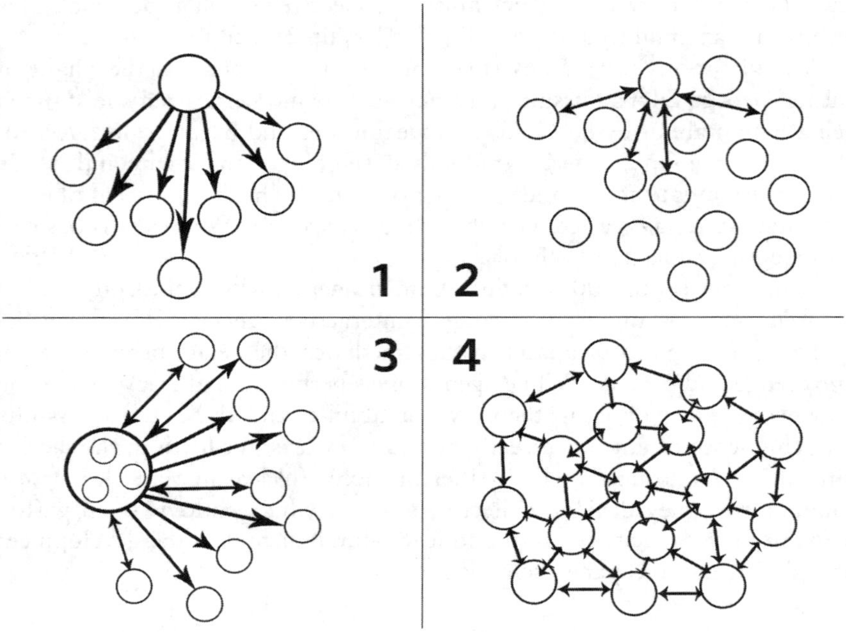

LEADERSHIP CAPACITY AS A PERSONAL CONSTRUCT

While previous texts on leadership capacity (Lambert, 1998, 2003) refer to the concept as an organizational construct, the idea involves significant individual capacity building as well. What is the leadership capacity of a particular person? A specific teacher? An individual citizen? During the past 15 years, scores of research studies have been framed around leadership capacity as a personal concept. These endeavors have enriched practice and resulted in substantial attention to teacher leadership preparation, support, professional development designs, and academies (see below and Chapter 3). In truth, leadership capacity is an interdependence of organizational and personal dimensions of participation and skillfulness.

Individual leadership capacity is enhanced, claim Stoll and Jackson (2009), by opportunities to engage in collaborative inquiry projects, co-planning with colleagues, leading community projects, and working with student leaders. Organizationally, these authors extol the benefits of shared decisionmaking, leadership teams, collective action and responsibility, and leadership capacity.

INTERVENTIONS DESIGNED TO FOSTER LEADERSHIP CAPACITY

Well-tailored intervention strategies create and expand both organizational and personal leadership capacity by simultaneously building leadership skills and broadening participation. Nestled in this vortex is the creation of trust essential to the emergence of integrated, networked systems (Image 4 above). Interventions involve structures and protocols that facilitate reciprocal patterns of interaction and the concomitant skills, understandings, and knowledge.

As noted by Jones et al. (2014) above, such interventions involve the collaborative skills and understandings essential to the building of leadership capacity. The need for participants to build capacity for group facilitation should not be understated. When navigating the challenging journey from low to high leadership capacity, there is bound to be conflict. Effective collaboration depends on how participants negotiate these rough terrains (Garmston & Zimmerman, 2013b).

Negotiating these terrains is neither an easy nor a smooth process. Jeffrey Stec (personal communication, May 10–15, 2015), executive director of Citizens for Civic Renewal in Cincinnati, tells a story, one of many:

> Despite 90 minutes of cooperative, small-group dialogue, tensions spilled over when the director of gifted services presented her plan for the following year to 35 angry parents. As the neutral facilitator, I empathized with the parents, discovered why they felt that way, and then asked that they "reframe their complaints as requests" in order to define the kind of future relationship they wanted with the director. This was easy enough work for a trained, independent, community-building facilitator. But when everyone had left the room and the director practically fell on me in an exhausted hug, I realized this type of meeting wasn't business as usual for a central office administrator.

Stec further observed: "I've found that the vast majority of administrators are great at their jobs, and many are very good team leaders who can organize a bureaucracy to get things done. Very few have developed the personal or professional skills to successfully manage whole system collaboration where 'everyone leads.'"

Interventions in Low Leadership Capacity Schools

Such complications as Stec described above are front and center in the intervention designs considered herein. In a low leadership capacity school or organization, the predominant challenge is to break dependencies between those with formal authority and those without. Principals and teachers often form codependencies leading to behaviors of favoritism on one side and blaming and avoiding on the other. Dependencies also can exist among teachers: "I trust you to be like me. When I blame and complain in the faculty room, I expect you to do the same." Targets of blame are administrators, parents, students, and the "unfair world." A principal can exercise effective strategies in such a school by establishing structures and protocols for visioning, collaboration, trust building, and employing the language of problem solving, rather than giving or withholding permission. However, the authors have found when teachers in low leadership capacity schools have an opportunity to work in high leadership capacity schools (or principals have an opportunity to work in similar districts), they more often behave as engaged and committed professionals. Thus, it is primarily a controlling culture that creates low capacity attitudes and behaviors, undesirable traits of which nearly everyone is capable.

While an initial glance at Figure 2.1 might suggest a linear movement from Archetype 1 to 2 (low to fragmented leadership capacity), this progression is rare. It is more likely that, with appropriate interventions, both Archetype 1 and 2 schools are more apt to become Archetype 3 (limited leadership capacity) schools on the path to the high leadership capacity school in Archetype 4. This shift represents significant progress in the journey toward improvement.

Interventions in Fragmented Leadership Capacity Schools

A fragmented leadership capacity school or organization has strikingly different challenges than a low leadership capacity school. Fragmented leadership cultures are found most often in medium-sized to large high schools. Programs can be islands of excellence or mediocrity. The range of quality is often breathtaking. Outstanding programs may exist as subcultures, with little interaction with the balance of the school. Resources are made available to these successful programs, often drawing these resources from areas of high need. In parallel existence with high-profile programs may be a substandard math program, tracking, and isolated classes for those perceived as having "less ability or potential." For the entrepreneurial advanced placement or calculus teacher, winning coach, music teacher, or debate instructor, the only students they may see are in their own programs.

Two helpful strategies include bringing the staff together as a whole to discuss, then dialogue about, a collective vision and goals for the school. An essential aspect of this journey—and often the most difficult—is to confront all staff members with data revealing poor performance by students who are "falling between the cracks." Such sobering data also may suggest, as they did in Santa Rosa, California, high schools, that a "three strikes and you're out" discipline mentality can create a fast track to incarceration.

Cross-disciplinary, skillful teams, most effectively vertical, can become the basis for in-depth conversations. A schoolwide leadership team draws together teacher leaders from across the school, leaders who are conscious of the discrepancies haunting its inhabitants. Multiple new leadership roles may be created to lead cross-disciplinary efforts (see the case of McNally High School, below). These approaches promise the growth of collaborative practice: enabling staff members to learn about and care about those who are not being served, and to trust one another to solve substantive problems. When done well, this is a portrait of significant school change.

Interventions in Limited Leadership Capacity Schools

Whatever route the school took to develop limited leadership capacity—often a stop on the road to high leadership capacity—a solid leadership group seeks to engage staff as a collective. The principal is not alone, but has close partners to design the journey ahead. The larger challenge here is that there are often hold-outs, those who want no part of this collaborative venture, or have tried it in the past and been wounded by its demise. These teachers may be discipline-bound, or just individuals who are unable to imagine another way of doing business. The challenge, in moving leadership capacity forward, is to enlarge the circle of participation, to engage the whole school community. It is essential that leadership group members not envision themselves as the primary decisionmakers (who then inform others of the decisions), for their role is to design how to engage others in collaborative learning, deliberation, and decisionmaking processes. This perspective changes the landscape of leadership communities.

Interventions in High Leadership Capacity Schools

Within a high leadership capacity school, the complex dynamic system is fostered and sustained by interdependent interactions among skilled, trusting adults and maturing, involved students. Consider the network in Image 4 above. Note the multitude of interactions. Situate the principal in any interior circle. When this web of interactions is in place, it is alive, dynamic, and reciprocal. Members have a sense of collective agency and will. Professionals, parents, and students share a mutual regard and respect. They can challenge the assumptions held by one another. The now-familiar processes involve visioning, learning, coaching, inquiry, dialogue, reflection, and action. The net result of these processes, acting in concert, is emergent and offers new experiences and practices. These are the self-organizing interactions that enable emergence into complex dynamic systems—living networks—now capable of being sustained. Why? The system and the individuals within it have transformed themselves through a spiral of interdependent relationships. In order to avoid fragmentation, each individual in the network needs to be fully aware of the whole set of leadership community agreements so they remain coherently present. Any one person, no matter his or her role, can leave, and the network closes once again, thus sustaining itself.

Throughout this text, we address the strategies for designing and fostering high leadership capacity schools and organizations capable of sustainability. Several factors must be in place for high leadership capacity schools to sustain their work over time. For instance, if a principal leading such an effort is transferred too early in the process—before certain factors such as shared leadership are in place—the effort can fall apart (Lambert, 2003). It is not uncommon for a politically chaotic and performance-challenged school or district to retreat to a more regressive stage than before the processes of improvement began.

THE ROLE OF THE PRINCIPAL IN FOSTERING LEADERSHIP CAPACITY

Selecting the best principal for a school slated to move into sustainable, high leadership capacity is one of the most challenging tasks for superintendents, school boards, and personnel directors (Fink, 2000; Hargreaves, 2005). Policies that aim to appoint formal leaders who can facilitate such improvements in the school culture need to be based on a full awareness of the path ahead.

That path is one of calibrating the amount of direct guidance needed initially, with an eye to shifting power and authority more broadly as staff members become skillful leaders. Such a principal needs the wisdom to let go of authority as others begin to participate in responsible ways. This is an educator who can calibrate and lead a faculty to a place of greater agency and adult development. This may appear antithetical to the shared, open leadership approaches indicated by the work in leadership capacity. However, the authors have found that in a low or fragmented leadership capacity school, certain agreements, protocols, shared goals, and trust need to be in place in order to advance the process of liberating leadership capacity. Well-tailored intervention strategies create and expand both organizational and personal leadership capacity.

Figure 2.3 specifies stages of development in this process. This figure was created as a result of a comprehensive, nationwide study of high leadership capacity schools and the struggles they encountered on the path toward improvement (Lambert, 2009). The figure was informed by the data and verified by the 12 researchers involved in the study. The stages delineated in the figure suggests the principal initially may play a more active role in establishing improvement designs, then gradually let go as relationships shift to reciprocity and shared work.

Figure 2.3. Principal Behaviors in Leadership Capacity Development

Instructive Stage *Principal as teacher, sponsor, facilitator*	Transitional Stage *Principal as guide, coach, and facilitator*	Liberating Stage *Principal as colleague, critical friend, mentor*
Personal attributes and behaviors: • Learns continually • Thinks strategically • Value/vision driven • Sets norms with staff • Supervises/ensures staff accountability • Convenes conversations • Honors history • Sponsors staff growth • Accepts responsibility • Breaks dependencies • Clarifies roles • Articulates strategies • Involves others in decisionmaking • Creates safe, "holding" environment	Personal attributes and behaviors: • Learns—attends to epiphanies • Thinks strategically • Translates values into vision language • Lets go, provides support, and sticks around • Scaffolds with ideas and questions • Mediates roles • Develops structures that build reciprocal relationships • Coaches for instructional improvement	Personal attributes and behaviors: • Learns continually • Thinks strategically • Value/vision driven • Continues and expands behaviors initiated in earlier phases • Coaches and mentors staff, parents, and community members • Self-evaluates (at all stages)
Instructs staff (or arranges for instruction) in: • collaboration, group processes, and teaming • conversation and dialogue • inquiry/data use • trust building • best instructional practices • communication skills • facilitation • conflict resolution • accountability • brokering information	Guides staff to: • develop a shared vision • establish process for observation of norms • participate in leadership • use inquiry • question assumptions • conduct constructivist conversations • identify and solve problems • surface/mediate conflict • find resources (time, professional development, monies) • plan strategically • broker information and knowledge	Participates with other members of the community to: • think holistically • share concerns/issues • share decisions • monitor and implement shared vision • engage in reflective practices (reflection/inquiry/dialogue/action) • monitor norms and take self-corrective action • build a culture of interdependency • self-organize • diversify and blend roles • broker knowledge • establish criteria for self-accountability • share authority and responsibility • plan for enculturation of new staff and succession

The Principal in a Low Leadership Capacity School

Aretha Madison, principal of Oak Valley Middle School, described in Chapter 1, encountered a low leadership capacity school when she arrived 3 years earlier. She came to this traditional school from a more progressive school where she had served as a teacher leader. Fresh out of a pioneering administrative credential program, she possessed ideas and practice in developing leadership capacity. As the oldest daughter in a single-parent family, Aretha possessed a strong sense of self-confidence, yet often battled with her natural tendencies to take charge. Since her mother had worked two jobs, she was often in charge of her younger siblings. The first in her family to go to college, it was with great pride that she had accepted her first teaching job, where she volunteered often and proved herself a tireless and eager learner. She was thrilled when her hard work paid off and she was chosen as the new principal at Oak Valley.

Aretha confessed in her diary: "I realize Oak Valley has had some autocratic principals and it would be easy for me to fall into that pattern too. But this isn't going to happen! I know I must develop a leadership community here—and that is what I plan to do." The pages of her diary filled through the first months of her tenure in the new assignment. She often had to talk herself down from being too directive—or from giving up. Fortunately, the district assigned her a mentor, a woman who had taught her in one of her graduate classes at the local university.

Aretha had learned that fostering leadership capacity in a low capacity school required a principal who could break dependencies, create collective structures, and begin the process of building agency. But how would she proceed? She knew she would need to be prepared to lead staff members away from dependence on authority and engage these individuals in collaborative work and key decisions in order to reverse the blaming, dysfunctional culture (see Figure 2.3, Instructive Stage). Aretha decided to open the conversation in this way: "I'm here on a journey—a journey to work together with you to create a community, a strong group of professionals who trust and learn from one another. I want you to join me in this journey." Until relationships and collaboration began to evolve to higher levels of actualization, she would be introducing and demonstrating new strategies—and providing opportunities for everyone to learn together. Performing leadership acts together is essential, and the process can get messy, but with dedicated focus, shared performance as a team emerged.

The Principal in a Fragmented Leadership Capacity School

The principal of a fragmented leadership capacity school (Figure 2.3, Instructive Stage) needs to be able to find traction, generate a collective will, and engage staff in taking a sobering look at the students it is not serving. This can be a particularly difficult road, since so many staff members have been isolated in their practice. As noted above, many of the independent ventures are of high quality; others are not. Gathering an informal team of willing and influential teachers and enabling them to see what is possible for their school can launch the school on the path to greater capacity. This team should be broad and diverse, as it is important not to create more inside/outside polarities, but to build relationships and alliances. When teachers become fully conscious that the most needy students are not doing well, they most often commit to student performance as a moral imperative. However, to do so without a growing sense of agency may result in finger pointing. The key approach here is to unify the culture and create a vision-oriented, collaborative school focused on the success of all students.

The Principal in a Limited Leadership Capacity School

The principal of a limited leadership capacity school no longer stands alone. He or she is joined by a few strong teacher leaders, who can become frustrated with those who remain obstinate to change. It is important that these individuals inspire and support one another while they learn to enlarge the circle of participation. A limited leadership capacity school culture (Figure 2.3, Transitional Stage), while the most advanced condition along the road to high leadership capacity, is often one of the more delicate. It is tempting for a principal to get involved with a skillful leadership team and join them in criticizing those who cross their arms and stay on the outside, resisting collaboration. An essential approach is to broaden the scope of involvement through whole-school strategies and designs, mentoring, team development, and incentives, thereby going to scale (Blankstein, Houston, & Cole, 2009; Lambert, 2003).

The Principal in a High Leadership Capacity School

For a new principal who has helped foster or has inherited a high leadership capacity school, the challenge is to perform as a valued leader among leaders (Figure 2.3, Liberating Stage). Fortunately, she or he is met with a number of gifts: a mature, engaged faculty with a strong sense of agency; structures involving staff, students, and parents in authentic ways; a powerful, practice-based vision; and successful or continually improving student performance. This new principal must guard against rushing in with a new reform agenda. The challenges of sustainability are quite different here than when a different principal is brought in to "single-handedly" reform a school (always an error). The new principal needs to learn what makes the school culture successful and seek to strengthen and deepen those factors.

At the same time, he or she needs to be aware of the dangers of burnout that can arise in high leadership capacity schools, and create a rhythm of efforts to punctuate hard work with reflective and relaxing interludes.

Throughout the process of fostering leadership capacity, the principal is a weaver of the network fabric, a catalyst who joins hands and practices, sustains pressure (i.e., keeps commitments on the table, ever present) and support, and uses the language of vision in conversations and written documents. In a high leadership capacity network, each participant becomes a weaver, alert to how connections are made and consensus is sustained. Each node (a person) of the network remains attentive to the need to provide sustenance to the other nodes. Such relationships arise when deep learning involves critical friendships, peer coaching, mentoring, and sustained mutually held high expectations. Unless both professional and psychic needs can be addressed through the network, it may unravel. This is especially true if in the past teachers were dependent on someone in a position of formal authority for praise, focus, and feedback.

It is also important to encourage and keep the door open to collaborative innovation to move the learning edge forward. Ideally, the new principal may have been a teacher within this very school.

Dale Skoreyko, principal of McNally High School in Calgary, Alberta, Canada, described his school's journey toward leadership capacity. Initially a school organized traditionally with department chairs in core subject areas, the first move toward rethinking these leadership roles was to integrate and link curricular areas. Newly networked roles included Classroom Technologies, Classroom Assessment, Inclusive Learning, and Instructional Processes. The roles of the three assistant principals were redesigned into discrete areas. Soon, it became apparent that many teachers were still waiting for direction from these leaders.

The McNally administrative team, upon reading Lambert's (1998, 2003) books on leadership capacity and *The Starfish and the Spider* by Brafman and Beckstrom (2006), realized that the designated-leader approach actually was inhibiting the initiative of others by causing the designated leader to be seen as the "go to" person. *What to do?* McNally High dissolved the designated department chair program, flattened the organization (eliminating the middle rows of appointed leaders), and set about developing the leadership skills of all teachers (Dale Skoreyko, personal communication, June 2–20, 2015).

Pam Luttrull is a Texas principal who utilizes the ESEA Turnaround Principles as a guide for school reform. These principles involve principal leadership, teacher and instructional quality, a redesigned school day, use of student performance data, a safe environment, and parent and community engagement. Pam learned that teacher leadership was the key to improving her school and sustaining those improvements. She told us:

Fortunately, I have learned that my greatest assets as a principal are already working within the school walls—the faculty and staff. My objective is to identify and encourage talented instructors to refine and encourage their talents and instructional prowess. I seek out opportunities to promote mentoring of novice teachers and collaboration among the faculty that builds a diverse panel of content experts to provide dynamic campuswide peer support. Even in my absence, campus leadership is always present. (Personal communication, May 10, 2015)

Pam's magical phrase might well be, "Even in my absence, campus leadership is always present." Teacher leadership is the key to developing and sustaining leadership capacity.

THE ROLE OF TEACHER LEADERS IN
FOSTERING LEADERSHIP CAPACITY

Pioneers in the field of teacher leadership established the urgency of the idea while also reframing the concept. Collay (1997, 2011) argued that teaching is leading. Teaching and leading, she noted, echo each other: Both require the engagement of students and colleagues; both call for skill and understandings in communication, inquiry, and reflection. Moller and Pankake (2006) invited educators to understand teacher leadership as a function of relationships, professional learning, and the redistribution of power and authority. Krovetz and Arriaza, in *Collaborative Teacher Leadership: How Teachers Can Foster Equitable Schools* (2006), argued that the skillful leadership of teachers and administrators is a prerequisite for any school focused on the expectation that all students will learn to use their minds and hearts well. The authors share the voices of teacher leaders drawn from exit portfolios from the master's program in collaborative leadership at San Jose State University. These insights are consistent with current perspectives on leadership. By broadening the scope and definition of leadership, others are invited in.

Yet, this can be a rough journey. When Ryan Land, former principal of R. D. Parker Collegiate in Thompson, Manitoba, envisioned the path toward teacher leadership, he wasn't surprised at the initial resistance. "I'm not a leader," insisted some teachers. Protecting the turf of department heads was the prime concern in this high school. Ryan used the lure of Chicago and an ASCD conference to build relationships and engage in professional learning together. The team bonded and launched their journey toward leadership capacity. In Chapter 6, the thorny terrain encountered by Ryan Land is described.

In 2011, Northside Elementary School, with a new principal, began a 2-year transition from a principal-centered school to a shared leadership school (Westsmith, 2014). Since Westsmith had been a teacher in a self-governing school (a school without a principal) in the same district, the staff invited her to Northside in hopes she could lead them from a principal-centered school to a shared leadership school. As the new principal, she followed the framework for leadership capacity (Lambert, 2003) and relational trust (Louis et al., 2010; Shannon & Bylsma, 2007) in working with staff to create a shared leadership school.

Westsmith sought to evaluate the effects of shared leadership on perceived staff transformations by extracting features from leadership capacity surveys (Lambert, 2003). As the Northside staff members fully engaged in leadership, both their attitudes and behaviors showed significant growth in leadership capacity. The study revealed a 90% or more growth rate in staff perception of the presence of these elements: (1) a shared vision, developed jointly, resulting in program coherence; (2) new roles and actions reflecting broad involvement, collaboration, and collective responsibility; and (3) reflective practice consistently leading to innovation (Westsmith, 2014). Relational trust among colleagues enabled the staff to tackle barriers and unmask assumptive thinking.

Within 2 years of the transition to shared leadership, student performance at Northside significantly shifted, earning the school the California Distinguished School Award. The award commended the school's shared leadership and program coherence. Student achievement was evidenced by a rise in the Academic Peformance Index (API) from 787 in 2011–12 to 837 in 2012–2013. (The API, which was instituted by the California legislature in 1999 as a component of the Public Schools Accountability Act, ranges from 200 to 1000.)

Teacher leadership and parallel shifts in principal leadership constitute the heart of high leadership capacity. At Northside, as in other high capacity schools, leadership among all participants, including students, parents, and community members, was necessary to establish the shift in student performance and school culture.

STUDENT AND PARENT LEADERSHIP

Students develop and learn in environments where teachers do the same. Adult leaders who build the leadership capacity of their schools create learning environments and experiences for students that elicit cultures of learning and positive involvement. Such environments lead to student resiliency and equitable achievement gains across diverse groups.

How do students emerge as learners and leaders? The same approaches that foster adult leadership also advance student learning—since leadership is a form of learning. We make the following assumptions to parallel those concerning adults:

- All children have the right, responsibility, and capability to be leaders.
- Learning communities should be designed to evoke leadership from all children.
- Leading is a public expression of learning.
- The historical mission of developing an educated citizenry for a democratic society is a function of early learning and leadership. (Lambert, 2003, pp. 55–56)

A student leader is one who has found his or her own voice and sense of agency, contributes to the world around him or her, and understands that his or her future is integral to the success of the community and society. Stoll and Jackson (2009) argue that "student leadership is a great untapped source of talent and energy in a school community" (p. 72).

At Oak Valley Middle School, student leadership is now a daily occurrence. Students participate on leadership teams, rotate leadership tasks in collaborative classrooms, and expect humane policies in restorative justice. Restorative justice means the involvement of the offending student in resolving and repairing harm done to others or the community—rather than using blanket punishments such as suspension and expulsion. The result is strengthened resilience and confidence through respectful participation and accepting responsibility for one's own behavior.

At Northside Elementary, parents are considered part of the staff; they are included in faculty meetings and welcomed into the faculty room and classrooms. These parents stepped up to implement a student recognition program to support a stagnant accelerated reader program, increasing the participation rate from 16% in 2011 to 78% in 2013. This program also strengthened the technological home–school connection, giving parents access to classroom data on student progress.

The authors advocate for a parent community that co-leads, participates, and assumes collective responsibility, such as in the case of Northside. Four key areas include the following:

- **Co-lead** with children, teachers, administrators, and other parents with regard for all children in the school (not just their own);
- **Participate** in education practices with others in the school community;
- **Advocate** for education with other parents, community, and policymakers; and
- **Assume** collective responsibility for the learning of all children. (Lambert, 2003, p. 66)

Figure 2.4 describes the desired shift from traditional to reciprocal roles. When parents are just customers to be accommodated or satisfied, a major resource for the school is lost. All too often they stand on the outside making demands instead of being engaged as partners. The current nationwide

Figure 2.4. Parents as Partners

Traditional Roles	Reciprocal Roles
Customers to be satisfied	Partners to be engaged
Servants to the school	Collaborators with staff and students
Obstacles to change	Facilitators of change
Critics to be persuaded	Colearners
Students of "parenting"	Coteachers
Audience for staff decisions and actions	Decisionmakers with staff
Fundraisers	Resource developers
Clerks and carpenters	Team members

Adapted from Lambert (2003). © 2003 by ASCD (www.ascd.org). Reprinted with permission.

conflicts over excessive testing are both an example and a consequence of the lack of school–community partnerships. Parents who find themselves consistently separated from policymakers and administrators may consider their only tactic to be to use a resistance strategy such as keeping students home on testing days. If parents are thoroughly involved, there might be a different outcome in decisionmaking at the state and national levels about testing: Assessments might be more multidimensional and integrated with instruction.

The realignment of relationships in schools and organizations is essential to the fostering of leadership capacity. Such realignment that involves reciprocal, networked, and collaborative relationships significantly alters the way in which schools work. Participants are supported in a co-leading, cooperative culture promoting learning for all.

CONCLUSION

Leadership capacity is liberated in school and district cultures by creating the conditions through which the patterns of interaction stimulate the emergence of vision-oriented, collaborative cultures. Such cultures are achieved through leadership defined as *fostering capacity in complex, dynamic systems through purposeful, reciprocal learning.*

The following six approaches are among those of high importance in the establishment of leadership capacity:

1. Where possible, hire personnel with the interest and inclination to do high capacity leadership work. Interview formats, a rubric, and surveys are available in Lambert (2003).
2. Seek every opportunity to build and strengthen relationship networks. Get to know one another; build teams and trusting relationships.

3. Self-assess staff and school capacity for leadership (e.g., using surveys, interviews, and dialogue).
4. Organize the school community for leadership work.
5. Develop a culture of inquiry by continually conversing, challenging assumptions, and inquiring in order to develop a shared knowledge base.
6. Collaboratively develop adaptive district policies that support leadership capacity.

The next chapter describes approaches to professional learning designed to liberate leadership capacity through continuous learning and leadership. Design principles and features create a framework for organizations that fosters leadership capacity through the complex, dynamic processes of purposeful, reciprocal learning. Programs and initiatives for professional learning are chosen to meet these criteria. Professional learning, coupled with student learning, creates the momentum essential for capacity building and sustainability.

QUESTIONS FOR REFLECTION

1. Assess your school or district based on Figure 2.1. As appropriate, circle features, in all four archetypes, that are present in your organization. Do you observe a tendency to function more closely to one archetype than another? In two archetypes more than others? What additional information would you need in order to assess your school more accurately?
2. Select the archetype in Figure 2.1 and the image in Figure 2.2 that you now consider to be closest to your school. You have been asked to serve on the new principal selection committee. Identify three to five selection criteria you would suggest to the committee.
3. Higher levels of leadership capacity help a school or organization become vision centered, challenge assumptions about effectiveness, and self-organize. How might an observer recognize such changes emerging in a culture?
4. Student leadership is indeed a rich, untapped resource. In groups of four, ask each participant to choose one of the following approaches (or offer one of his or her own) and discuss why the ideas might invite students into leadership: mentoring, cross-age tutoring, journaling, classroom collaboration, participation in leadership teams, restorative justice programs, serving on community boards and councils, outward bound.
5. How does your school or district work with parents? Examine Figure 2.4 and imagine the two columns as continua. Assess your school's work with parents. Discuss.

CHAPTER 3

Designing Professional Learning Cultures

Since all individuals, organizations, and societies have capacities for leadership, professional learning is the foremost feature in the liberation of leadership capacity. This assertion requires equitable, skillful, and collaborative participant engagement. Acquiring the skills, processes, knowledge, and deep understandings needed to create and sustain high leadership capacity organizations is the work of a professional learning culture.

This chapter describes designs, frameworks, and components for professional learning in high leadership capacity organizations. Such learning involves the reciprocal processes of leadership, most specifically, inquiry, reflection, and discourse. In professional learning cultures, participants grow in their capacities to self-author their professional lives, just as the community—in parallel—evolves into collective agency. This is a reciprocal process, undertaken in concert. Complex and dynamic, such processes establish emergence, a condition leading to self-organization—the belief in the transformative capacity of a community. Transformative cultures search for a consilience of principles and actions, drawing from multiple knowledge fields—complex systems theory, design thinking, adult learning and development, neurobiology, and constructivist learning and leadership theories.

In order to build high leadership capacity organizations, professional learning must be intentionally created so learners become the developers and leaders in the design process. This redesign needs to cultivate a culture that promotes an "entrepreneurial spirit" (Martin & Osberg, 2007; Zhao, 2012), an impulse for leadership. At the core of an entrepreneurial spirit are characteristics of inspiration, creativity, focus, courage, and the willingness to persist. This spirit creates the compelling desire to meet the needs of all learners and to participate in the design and construction of one's own learning.

MAJOR DESIGN PURPOSES FOR PROFESSIONAL LEARNING

The approaches suggested in this chapter invariably result in higher student test scores—but that is not the primary or singular focus here. The goal, more ambitious, is to create rich environments and learning conditions that develop diverse talents, passions, and collective intelligence and agency. According to Thomas and Brown in *A New Culture of Learning: Cultivating the Imagination for a World of Constant Change* (2011), today's learning culture comprises two elements: The first is unlimited access to information and resources in order to follow passions, experiment, and play; the second is an environment in which both structure and boundaries allow for experimentation and building agency. Both of the elements fused together produce an engaging environment for learning.

Daniel Pink (2005) suggests that such engaging environments contain the essentials of "high-concept, high-touch" (pp. 65–66)—the right ingredients for creating professional learning cultures and studios, in which this spirit flourishes. Pink suggests that these ingredients are: design, story, symphony, empathy, play, and meaning. Conceptual designs composed of such elements are physically beautiful and emotionally transcendent; compelling narratives are told, and disparate pieces are brought together like harmonic compositions. In these environments, participants seek to understand and care for others, forging patterns of relationships essential to growing leadership capacity.

In this chapter, four major purposes guide the designs for professional learning cultures. Organizations increase leadership capacity through the following:

1. New professional learning designs
2. Professional learning in high leadership capacity organizations
3. Leadership skills and participation in high leadership capacity organizations
4. Recognizing and learning from exemplary programs

NEW PROFESSIONAL LEARNING DESIGNS

A multiplicity of designs leads to high leadership capacity. These designs emerge out of organizational purposes, structures, and patterns of interactions within organizations and societies. When professionals are learning together in continuous reciprocal relationships, "a learning culture emerges and grows through the cultivation and development of creative, intellectual, and moral faculties" (Thomas & Brown, 2011, p. 37). Perspectives of constructivist leaders are those of professionals with "growth mindsets, the belief that basic qualities can be cultivated through effort" (Dweck, 2006, p. 7). The idea that learning is lifelong is now a given. The how, what, where, and even who of professional learning are changing.

"What" is to be learned depends on the organization's and individual's stage of leadership capacity development. But in all cases, the "how" and "where" people learn are flexible and open to change. The "who" arises from the assumption of constructivist leadership that all members, and the organization as a whole, have the right, capacities, and responsibility to learn and lead. An assessment of the organization's stage of leadership capacity development (low to high leadership capacity; see Figure 2.1) and the choice of the design process influence the what, how, and where for professional learning.

A conventional view of staff development as a transferable package of knowledge to be distributed to teachers in small pieces by experts or consultants has needed radical transformation and rethinking for a long time (Darling-Hammond, 2013; Hargreaves, 2003; Lambert, 1988; Lieberman & Miller, 1991). These old assumptions have been slow to change. Archaic thinking about professional learning carries limited conceptions about how learning occurs. It typically is grounded in a set of assumptions about educators, teaching, leading, and the process of change that does not match what is now known about adult learning, neurobiology, and complex systems theory. With the advent of design thinking as collaborative, creative problem solving and innovation, educators are revolutionizing professional learning events (e.g., blended and personalized learning, podcasts, just-in-time online learning) into high capacity professional learning cultures.

The Every Student Succeeds Act incorporates many of these newer understandings of professional learning. Stephanie Hirsh, executive director of Learning Forward (2015), expressed her approval of wording in the measure that defines educator learning as "an integral local strategy for building educator capacity to help students succeed with high academic standards." Just as important, she notes, is that "professional development must be 'sustained,' intensive, collaborative, job-embedded, data-driven and classroom-focused" (Learning Forward, 2015). This chapter describes professional learning consistent with the new policy.

Design Thinking: Collaborative, Innovative Processes

Design thinking in education is still evolving. However, the fundamental aspects include collaboration, diverse points of view, and integrated thinking. David and Tom Kelley (2013), authors and founders of IDEO (www. ideo.com/expertise/education), an award-winning global design firm, were instrumental in the development of design thinking methodologies. Such designs unlock the natural ability of people to use their imaginations to create. Being creative, those authors suggest, means generating new ideas and having the courage to experiment. Design thinking provides structures and processes to support open, honest, safe environments for problem solving and for innovating, challenging assumptions, and generating multiple possibilities. This mindset establishes the expectation that everyone can be part of creating a more desirable future.

The five-part IDEO design cycle begins with discovery focused on challenges, personal interpretations, and the chance to design through ideation, experimentation, and evolution. For example, the Ormandale Elementary School in Portola Valley, California, set up a design process to explore students as shapers of knowledge rather than receivers of knowledge. Through this process the teachers developed *A Guide to Investigative Learning* (2008). Using the IDEO approaches, they focused on inquiry, investigations, and reflection. In the process, learners recognized both what works and what does not; both became launching pads and scaffolds for the next learning cycle.

Design thinking is characterized by the natural tendencies to reflect, reorganize, reimagine, and re-create experiences (Ruttonsha & Quilley, 2014). These processes are democratic in that they respect differences in opinions and perceptions while collaboratively ensuring the expression of multiple visions that can fuse into shared visions. Design depends on creative energy flows arising when people build on one another's ideas. The approach contends that iterative, collaborative planning, decisionmaking, and envisioning processes promote broad participation. Such thinking heightens the capacity of communities and individuals to self-author their own professional learning and is applicable in all settings.

The Athenian School in Danville, California, utilized a design process originated by the Design School at Stanford University to create their own process for the creation of interdisciplinary, experiential courses. Course proposals are composed within guidelines consistent with the values and principles of the school. In the fall of 2015, The Politics of Disaster was offered for the first time. This new course, designed by April Smock in collaboration with a team of teachers, involves climate science, economics, structural and social engineering, and photography. The course was built on the stories of those impacted by disasters, including an examination of the long-term impact on their communities. Students studied the effects of Hurricane Katrina as a case study and then conducted individual interviews with survivors of the San Bruno pipeline explosion and the Richmond Chevron fire, as well as with a University of California, San Francisco, doctor who volunteered to provide medical care to earthquake victims in Haiti. Students toured the California Butte fire damage, interviewed fire victims and local East Bay Municipal Utility District employees, and worked on a local project to help area residents with their rebuilding efforts (personal communication, December 17, 2015).

In the spring of 2016, another new course emerged from the design process at Athenian called California Water: The Power and Beauty of Water in a Thirsty World. The course was codesigned by Kathleen Huntington and a small teaching team, and it examined the story of water in California, focusing on cultural and scientific contexts as students traversed natural and engineered waterscapes throughout the state to test, measure, photograph, and experience water in its various forms from the snowpack in the Sierras to the groundwater in the drought-stricken Central Valley (personal communication, December 18, 2015).

Federal, state, and regional governmental departments also use design thinking to solve problems, develop adaptive policies, respond to the needs of local districts and schools, and distribute resource support equitably. Educators, schools, and districts develop curriculum, assessments, lessons, and policy, and solve problems with design thinking strategies. Students independently use design thinking for project- and inquiry-based learning. As a natural approach for inquiry-based learning, design thinking begins by posing questions, identifying problems, or constructing scenarios. As more people learn and apply the structures and processes, creative thinking stimulates innovation. Design thinking builds individual and collective intelligence by enlisting all participants in the discovery of diverse solutions. Thus, when design thinking becomes an internalized habit of individuals and organizations, it creates conditions for transformational change.

Tensions between individual and organizational practice often challenge organizations to consider design processes in order to seek a coherent approach. When solutions and knowledge emerge from the wisdom of the whole, what participants are coming to know enables them to self-organize and coalesce around key options. High leadership capacity organization members regularly work to build professional knowledge through design. This fosters an interactive, dynamic professional learning culture in which learning becomes embedded into daily actions. The consulting group Tomorrow Makers uses design thinking routinely in their work and offers an example of how the design process works (see text box below).

In anticipation of widening interest and participation in design thinking, new methods and protocols, such as the approaches used in the Boston Library (see text box below) are being developed and implemented around the world. Links for educators to search for protocols, examples, and blogs about design thinking can be readily accessed on the web.

When professional learning cultures learn and practice design thinking for problem solving and innovation, they participate in dialogue, inquiry, and reflection to generate new neural networks. Therefore, in such cultures, the designs with the most promise are those that create a confluence of learner-centered approaches. Adult development theory is a fundamental consideration in design.

Designs for Adult Learning

Since adult learners engage in professional learning at different levels of development, or may follow different learning pathways, it is necessary that

---

DESIGN WITH TOMORROW MAKERS

In 2015, the nonprofit consulting group Tomorrow Makers joined with a subset of a large, diverse, and international community of participants from information services, libraries, and museums at Boston Library to explore and design the future of information services. The work was organized around the question: "What is our information future and how do we engage and design with it, helping pave a path for learners to understand the challenges and excel in their abilities to keep pace with the rate of change?" (Taylor, 2015, p. 2). Paper hung from every surface of a large, open room with dividers. During a 3-day experience, participants moved among fluid groups designing an information future with technology embedded in every facet. Words, illustrations, and constructed boxes (containers) revealed the ideas and possibilities for the future. Photographs memorialized the collective responses of smiles and laughter when breakthroughs occurred; furrowed brows expressed participants' struggles with bold ideas for inclusion, serving diverse community needs, the need for civic discourse, and lifelong learning. In the coming year, a volunteer group will produce a white paper detailing both the process and the plans for the future (see www.tomorrowmakers.org/journal).

---

they be involved in the planning, implementation, and assessment of their experiences. It is essential to keep in mind that the brain remains highly adaptive throughout life. Learning experiences gradually sculpt the physical architecture of the brain, modifying connections among neurons in specific areas. These areas are reorganized into an ever-changing schema. Connections used the most are strengthened and those less active are weakened or eliminated. Further, inspiring and supporting relationships activate the brain's openness to new ideas. This insight suggests a fundamental interdependence among the brain's social and emotional processing functions and other aspects of learning (Immordino-Yang, 2008).

Educators welcome confirmation of the importance, for both adults and children, of building cohesive environments where trust, satisfaction, and interest are ever present. Learning is strengthened when emotions and social interaction are integrated (Immordino-Yang, 2008; Immordino-Yang & Damasio, 2007). Planning for and paying attention to emotions embeds learning in memory, thereby stimulating deeper engagement. This understanding influences how professional learning experiences are designed.

In 1989, Sarah Levine, in her book *Promoting Adult Growth in Schools*, analyzed numerous developmental theories and stories and proposed some considerations for providing professional "development." These suggestions for designing professional learning cultures still hold true today. Levine argued that educators need to renew their skills and refocus their professional energies in order to maintain commitment and enthusiasm for their work. Renewal and refocus accompany shared work in supportive and collegial relationships, discovery of new facets of the teaching profession, and involvement in making decisions that affect educators' lives and work. In order to continue to develop and grow, adults need to maintain their sense of purpose and locus of control over their learning environments.

Throughout adulthood, both interactive and reflective experiences support adults' focus on intimacy, generativity, and integrity. Levine's work, and that of other adult development theorists, continues to inform the field of professional learning. These insights lead to the recommendation that major professional learning designs be responsive to the needs and development of individuals as well as to the systems in which they work—all creating a school culture that stimulates and continues adult development and building capacity.

Robert Kegan's (1982, 1994) constructive-developmental theory, expanded in collaboration with Lisa Lahey (2009) and further interpreted by educator Eleanor Drago-Severson (2009), proposes that the creation of personal identity and self-authoring continues throughout adulthood. Kegan's view of adult development defines four mindsets—each qualitatively more complex—which adults reveal as they respond to life's challenges. Level 1, the *institutional level*, is anchored by institutional knowledge; this mindset assumes someone else knows best. While many organizations espouse collaborative work, their policies often continue to reflect a top-down mindset: "Do as we direct." Level 2 is the *socializing level* in which individuals learn to subordinate their desires in order to get along. In socializing cultures, loyalties, power, and control may dominate, just as in a low leadership capacity school. This emphasis on accommodation is how many teachers work, either letting go and following along, or hiding their own sense of agency deep within. Indeed, it is one way teachers cope with dysfunctional leadership and cultures not supportive of teacher development. Because the past 20 years of reform have placed such a heavy emphasis on mandates, Level 3, *self-authoring*, is often difficult for educators to fully appreciate or achieve. Kegan believes that understanding how we own our work, are self-guided, and self-evaluate is the primary work of adulthood. Finally, Level 4, *transforming*, views the world as not having such clear boundaries and sees it as an interacting web of networks, an image keenly sought by a high leadership capacity school. As adults move through these stages, they do not lose the earlier understandings, but rather are able to assume a broader reflective consciousness about their relationships to the objective world. A person's level of complex thinking shapes how he or she understands roles and responsibilities in personal and community lives.

In his ideal world, Kegan (1982) described a "holding environment" (p. 116), which he defined as an environment that both supports and challenges adults through the increasing complexities of development. Work environments have the potential to be such holding environments. Raul's story represents a self-authored learning design embedded in a high leadership capacity school (see text box below). Oak Valley Middle School is a holding environment that supports Raul's path toward professionalism and leadership. His path was responsive to his own experience in a constructivist classroom in 7th grade, his interests, and the community goals of Oak Valley Middle School.

ONE TEACHER'S LEARNING JOURNEY

Raul, a first-year teacher, came to teaching with a passion to make a difference for middle school students. After a rigorous interview process, including a discussion with teachers about an article on teaching philosophy, a demonstration lesson, a portfolio review, and three different interviews with parents and students, Raul accepted an offer to teach at Oak Valley. By this time, the school had gained a statewide reputation for being innovative. During the interview process, he learned all the teachers were selected because they liked working with adolescents and wanted to work in a collaborative learning community.

After he was hired, Raul toured the school with one of the veteran science teachers, Alice. As they walked, he vividly remembered his own middle school experience in Los Angeles. "This is when I first thought of being a teacher," he told Alice. "My science teacher, Mrs. Garcia, opened the world of science for me through discovery learning. Tapping into my sense of wonder. Can you believe it—we are still in touch online." Alice smiled and listened deeply.

"Mrs. Garcia asked us to keep a portfolio of lab work and the questions we investigated," Raul continued. "We even kept photos and a journal— about the moon's movement in the sky, I recall. We had fun. Took risks. I can't wait to share with my students the importance of the moon to ancient civilizations. Mrs. Garcia even took us to the Mayan observatory in the Yucatan Peninsula. Turns out I'm part Mayan." "I'm glad you're here," Alice said. "Working with you will be a sheer pleasure."

Alice became Raul's coach and critical friend. Together with another science teacher and a history teacher, they applied to attend a summer workshop for teachers on design thinking at the Stanford School Lab network (www.nuevaschool.org/outreach/institutes-and-conferences/design-thinking-institute) in California. Raul's first year at Oak Valley proved to be an extraordinary learning experience in a community of dedicated professionals.

A story told by Patrice Bryan from the Maplewood Richmond Heights School District in St. Louis, Missouri, described teachers who were self-authoring and transforming in their views of teaching:

> I was in the Research and Design Center last week talking to the media specialist, Ms. Baker. She was trying to find a way to connect a new resource to a class, and said, "Oh, I think Rowley does a unit on Picasso." I said, "Oh yeah! That's a beautifully written unit." The truth is, much of our curriculum is pure artistry because it's nuanced with the expertise of our teachers, and each one brings something unique, creative, and often cosmopolitan to their curriculum. Notorangelo doesn't just teach a foreign language; she lived in Honduras and served in the Peace Corps, immersing herself in developing-world Spanish. Rowley didn't just write a unit on Picasso; he's studied art and brings that unit to life with a deep understanding of the intersection of art and literature. Our teachers are hardworking—that's a given—but even better for our kids and their learning, our teachers have grand life experiences. They bring this experience and a passion for their subjects to the classroom. (Personal communication, December 12, 2015)

In Maplewood Richmond Heights, life experiences and passion are a natural part of the environment. Confident it will move educators to higher levels of development earlier in their personal and career lives, organizations increasingly are giving substantial attention to such learning environments. Patrice Bryan lived her professional life immersed within an environment that created opportunities to reach transformational levels of development.

Drawing from knowledge about design thinking, the brain's capacities for learning, and adult development, Figure 3.1 proposes professional learning design principles as a promising path toward high leadership capacity organizations.

PROFESSIONAL LEARNING IN
HIGH LEADERSHIP CAPACITY ORGANIZATIONS

Communities are the design contexts for professional learning. The term *professional* may suggest a role apart—apart from those who are not certified to teach or serve in formal leadership roles. The intention is otherwise. This chapter is about learning that leads to high leadership capacity. Consequently, the approaches herein are essential in the school community as a whole and the broader world as well. A student group travels to Peru to build a greenhouse for a small village; another travels to Czech Republic to

Figure 3.1. Professional Learning Principles

1. Employ design thinking to create programs, environments, and cultures that provide for a clear sense of purpose allowing for interest and choice
2. Promote collaborative involvement, reciprocal relationships, reflection, and inquiry
3. Foster renewal of skills, an internal locus of control, and respect for personal identity
4. Provide unlimited information, resources, and experience to provoke creativity and innovation
5. Construct a holding environment that provides for psychological safety, trust, loose boundaries, and time for learning
6. Adopt processes for collaborative visioning and decisionmaking

---

remodel an orphanage, or to Cuba to assist with organic farming. Teachers and parents go along. The skills and understandings in this chapter prepare each of these adventurers well for the worlds they'll meet, for every community, every culture provides foundational interactions for emergence.

Participatory Democracies: Communities as Learning Contexts

When professional learning cultures display the conditions of participatory democracies, all members of the community are encouraged to make meaningful contributions as equal members through involvement in decisionmaking, problem solving, and envisioning. Organizations conscientiously organized in this way adopt skills, attitudes, and beliefs that are responsive to multiple perspectives and the diverse needs of individuals within the organization.

Participatory structures and processes in democratic environments demonstrate the value of diversity and collaboration. Maxine Greene pointed out that democracy often is narrowly interpreted. She said, "We think too seldom about the connections in a democracy between freedom and relationships, literary and public dialogue, happiness and social concern" (Greene, 1995, p. 65). Linda Darling-Hammond (1997) suggested that educational places are social institutions charged with teaching democracy. Yet a critical disconnect can occur; these places rarely "teach democratically or enact democratic life. . . . They are more authoritarian than participative" (p. 141). Both Darling-Hammond and Greene—and John Dewey before them—advocated for school cultures that support democracy, which is the aim of high leadership capacity schools. In such schools, democracy is a way of living in and out of the classroom. Educators are active members of a democratic society, co-constructing strategies needed for problem solving and building inclusive, caring communities.

Communities and networks thrive in participatory democracies. Governance is flattened by design into panarchal structures, "interlinked in continual adaptive cycles of growth, accumulation, restructuring, and renewal" (Taylor & Johnson, 2009, p. 10). In panarchal systems, reflective practice, inquiry, and reciprocal interactions are the norm. The interactions include conversations from which meaning and knowledge can be constructed, encouraging professionals to generate collective meaning and purpose grounded in practice (Lambert et al., 2002). In these environments, learning is continuous and leadership is the responsibility of everyone.

Learning Communities

Ensuring high participation in a skilled organization means that professional learning is integrated and occurs in community. Two primary types of learning communities are being used in education today. The one more commonly found is "professional learning communities" (PLCs), in which groups are designed for learning and researching by continuously thinking, reflecting, evaluating, and inquiring about practice to improve it (Annenberg Institute for School Reform [AISR], 2004; DuFour & Eaker, 1998; Hord, 1997; Stoll, Rolam, McMahon, Wallace, & Thomas, 2006). A major focus is student work, often characterized by test scores.

The second type of learning community is "communities of practice" (CoPs), in which groups emerge out of common interests and become co-participative social enterprises, considering learning as a social system. These communities provide social engagement as the proper context for learning (Lave & Wenger, 1991; Smith, 2003/2009; Wenger, 1998).

While either of these types of communities can be self-organizing, design thinking requires that a school or an agency take specific steps to create formal structures for incorporating those communities best suited to the local context. If an organization intends to incorporate either form of community into its learning culture, it is vital to analyze which design is the better match for its intended purposes. Both community approaches promote ongoing learning and improvement of practice, and in some contexts they overlap.

Over the past 20 years much has been written about these types of communities, using a variety of models. In a comprehensive review of communities, the AISR (2004) has outlined the effects of formal professional learning communities on learning cultures and provided a set of criteria for measuring their effectiveness. The critical characteristics of an effective PLC, AISR researchers claim, is that these learning communities are ongoing, embedded in a specific need in a particular setting, aligned with a reform initiative, and grounded in a collaborative, inquiry-based approach to learning (AISR, 2004, p. 1). Congruent with communities of practice is the idea of using exercises and newly acquired skills and knowledge "on a practice field" (Heifetz, Grashow, & Linsky, 2009, p.

9). These authors describe practice as those opportunities participants use as learning forums to gain knowledge and refine skills. Practice fields are pervasive and exist everywhere—in workrooms, meetings, classrooms, hallways, and play spaces. Effective learning communities involve skill in reflection, dialogue, and inquiry—the very skills essential in high leadership capacity settings. These skills lead to improved relationships, growth in knowledge, and collective agency. Henceforth the term *learning communities* will be used to identify this genre of professional learning, in which the participants are both learners and actors.

When learning communities include all members in decisionmaking, they provide opportunities for members to make meaningful contribution as leaders; and when they establish respectful working agreements, they are practicing participatory democracy. In these democracies, trusting relationships are built, visions are collectively created, and everyone is included in acquiring congruent collaborative skills, attitudes, processes, and behaviors. Democratic approaches are especially powerful when they embody the mindset that all people have agency and all are respected—when participants have authority to make choices in governance, designing, experimenting, and evaluating. Hillbrook School is an example of a democratic, high capacity learning culture.

A kindergarten through 8th-grade school in the Silicon Valley of California, Hillbrook takes seriously its responsibility for creating a participatory democracy; so much so that it recently added a statement of inclusivity to its core beliefs, mission, and vision statements: "Hillbrook is intentionally creating a diverse community, reflective of the diversity of Silicon Valley." To establish this commitment firmly into practice, the staff is consciously building "inclusive" mindsets by creating an environment where everyone, including students, has a voice. Inclusivity is a core focus, taking every opportunity to "hear, appreciate, and accept all voices and perspectives . . . preparing students to develop into responsible citizens in a global world." Inclusivity is one of the criteria used to measure decisions, curriculum, activities, and interactions with the broader community. The school seeks to understand and accept cultural, racial, socioeconomic, learning, sexual orientation, belief system, and gender differences. Thus, Hillbrook is a safe, comfortable place for children to learn about difference in themselves and others.

The HERO club at Hillbrook is a student group focused on supporting minority groups, including lesbian, gay, bisexual, and transgender children and adults. Students and teachers challenge ideas and behaviors that diminish others and use project-based curriculum and instruction as a means of analyzing social and intellectual problems from multiple perspectives. Hillbrook hired an inclusion coordinator, who leads the design of learning opportunities for staff and students, promoting diversity, equity, inclusion, and cultural competency, including supporting leadership opportunities for students as advocates for inclusion.

The Hillbrook mindset began 3 years earlier with the founding of a Center for Teaching Excellence. The center was designed to promote collaborative teaching, teacher development, and staff diversification. It attracted more than 20 new or early-career residential coteachers who work with experienced lead teachers, creating an immersive experience of practice, reflection, and study.

Mark Silver, head of school, says Hillbrook reflects the words of John Dewey: "a society of free individuals in which all, in doing each his own work, contributes to the liberation and enrichment of the lives of others" (personal communication, May 25–June 28, 2015).

LEADERSHIP SKILLS AND PARTICIPATION IN HIGH LEADERSHIP CAPACITY ORGANIZATIONS

Hillbrook School and the composite Oak Valley Middle School, and so many others like them, recognize the dynamic between high participation and skillfulness in high leadership capacity schools—and plan accordingly. Such schools accelerate changes by assessing their current status and choosing a forward developmental path. This path involves the professional learning principles described above as a framework for learning reflection, inquiry, and discourse, among other key leadership skills.

Figure 3.2 suggests a select number of cumulative leadership skills central to the movement from one archetype to another on the road to high leadership capacity. They represent skills and actions by principals in interaction with teachers and other colleagues, students, and community members; and by teachers in interaction with one another, administrators, students, and parents.

The skills and actions in Figure 3.2 are selected for their particular strength in leveraging leadership capacity. Skills in communication and collaboration are presented more fully in Chapter 4. These tools are vital to conversations in design thinking and for collaborative work. All of the skills suggested are important in building trusting relationships and challenging old assumptions. However, three skill domains are particularly powerful: reflection, inquiry, and dialogue. All three interconnected elements lead to the examined life worth living. The dynamic is envisioned in Figure 3.3.

Imagine these three elements in motion and in any order. The movement spirals deeper and deeper, revealing underlying assumptions, surfacing and examining thought, activating metacognition. Faculty members at a high school in northern Alberta, Canada, posed this compelling question: "Why

Figure 3.2. Learning Paths from Low to High Leadership Capacity

Low Leadership Capacity (Archetype 1):

- Find a focus and accept shared responsibility
- Create working agreements for collaboration
- Experience autonomy and discretion in order to break dependencies
- Broadly share in problem solving and decisionmaking
- Share lessons in grade-level teams, establish learning communities
- Learn skills in dialogue, inquiry, and reflection

Fragmented Leadership Capacity (Archetype 2):

- Collaborate and discuss schoolwide issues in vertical teams, develop learning communities
- Convene schoolwide meetings for shared decisionmaking
- Examine student performance data to address learning gaps and underachievement
- Use design thinking to plan schoolwide professional learning
- Encourage use of narrative/stories to deepen understanding of all students and families
- Share teaching lessons and strategies in various teams

Limited Leadership Capacity (Archetype 3):

- Build effective leadership and vertical learning community teams
- Learn broad-based, inclusive leadership skills to encircle the circles of participation
- Use design thinking for problem solving and innovation
- Develop mentoring, coaching, and critical friend programs
- Initiate action research based on questions arising from dialogue
- Discover and join networks beyond the school

High Leadership Capacity (Archetype 4):

- Deepen leadership skills to ensure vision-oriented inquiry, dialogue, reflection, and action among all participants
- Internalize "entrepreneurial spirit" as a platform for innovation
- Secure a professional learning culture
- Expand relationships beyond local organizations, network broadly
- Memorialize work with illustrations, words, videos
- Create a work rhythm with interludes for play, individual reflections, celebration, and experiences in the outside world

Figure 3.3. Learning Dynamic in High Leadership Capacity Organizations

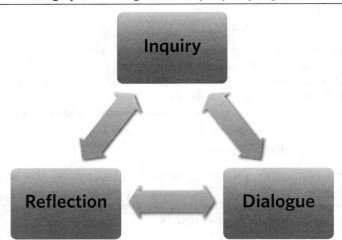

aren't we reaching our native students?" The group of educators entered into small-group dialogue—moments of intense chatter followed by interludes of silence. As the groups reported out, ideas flew onto the whiteboard. Then, one teacher admitted: "We really don't know, do we?" Another reflective silence followed. The facilitator led the group to pose their concerns as inquiry questions. What followed was 3 weeks of data collection by inquiry teams: Parents and students were interviewed, performance and discipline data were examined, classes were visited, and programs in other schools where native students were performing better were investigated. After the data were shared and understood, the school community redesigned itself. The new program allowed for attention to relationships through a 4-year advisory and mentor program; problem-based, active learning; broad-based student governance; and significant parent involvement.

Reflection in action, on action, and for action (Schon, 1983) helps educators and communities to be self-authoring and self-correcting. In the next chapter, dialogue is described as an elegant form of conversation characterized by listening, reflecting, and altering perceptions. Reflection in and on action creates new thinking processes while surfacing questions—questions ripe for further inquiry. Inquiry ranges in scope from the question itself to the investigated question in which information and data are sought. The profession has long referred to the "reflective practitioner" as one who possesses the mindset described in Figure 3.4. Reflective communities employ reflection, dialogue, and inquiry in a natural symphony of group expression. These are the reciprocal processes of leadership.

Figure 3.4. Profile of Reflective Professional Educators in a High Capacity System

- Commit to and assume responsibility for continuous learning as individuals and collectively
- Develop awareness of themselves, others, and contexts
- Develop the skills for design thinking and leadership
- Disconnect (break set) from old assumptions in order to form new understandings
- Adjust or change practice to align with new understandings
- View knowledge construction and acquisition as an ongoing, additive process

Adapted from York-Barr, Sommers, Chere, & Montie, 2006, p. 10.

Cathryn Smith, an assistant professor at Brandon University in Manitoba, Canada, created and studied leadership communities that exemplify reflective practice. In her dissertation study, Smith identified learning processes that foster agency and a concern for social justice issues: reflection through journaling, learning-focused dialogue, action research cycles, self-assessment, peer feedback, and critical reflection (2014). Smith now works with regions and schools throughout Canada and with professional preparation programs at her university to teach what she has learned (personal communication, June 1–10, 2015). These findings are consistent with the authors' understandings of leadership capacity.

RECOGNIZING AND LEARNING FROM EXEMPLARY PROGRAMS

In considering exemplary programs, the authors applied the professional learning principles described in Figure 3.1 and the leadership skills in Figure 3.2. These programs exist in schools, districts, regions, and states, and internationally. As systems move toward high leadership capacity, they create new or improved approaches to professional learning and practice. These exemplary programs include approaches that aspire to create leadership capacity and new teacher induction, with training provided through academies and learning centers. All foster collaborative learning. Many provide for the preparation of supportive coaches, mentors, and critical friends who are experienced colleagues, interested in building relationships with other professionals and seeking leadership roles.

Ohio Voices for Learning: A Reggio Emilia-Inspired Forum

This pioneering forum has established reflection, dialogue, and inquiry in a dynamic statewide network. Its purpose is to value, respect, and honor the diversity and integrity of all young children, their families, and the professionals who support them. This collaborative study group inspires high-quality early childhood Reggio Emilio learning communities. Through open, collegial relationships, conversations, and gatherings as researchers, they reflect on practice and advocate for inquiry-based learning for children. A few dialogue questions are: "How do we simultaneously follow the interests of children and meet district mandates? What organizational structures are needed to support working in a more collaborative, evolving way with children? How does structure support flexibility and responsiveness?"(ohiovoices.org). A part of the larger international Reggio Children program now in more than 34 countries, Ohio Voices supports a coherent constructivist approach to learning.

The New Teacher Center, Santa Cruz, California

A challenge in education today is to attract to and retain in our nation's schools the best possible teachers and administrators. The successful New Teacher Center (NTC) is a world leader in mentoring new teachers and new leaders. The center's purpose is to support novice teachers and leaders in an effort to stem the tide of losing the best and brightest in the profession. A small group of pioneers met in founder Ellen Moir's Santa Cruz garage around a card table and developed this organization. As the work grew and continued, the organization evolved from a new teacher project affiliated with a university into a national center, continuously experimenting and learning from best practices. As Betsy Warren, senior program consultant, reports, it began with new teacher induction and developed into best practices for principal induction and mentor development. NTC staff members consistently have learned from one another, from the field, and from current research. Staff members observe one another work and provide feedback, collaborate on projects, and set high standards for individual work and teamwork. Together they constitute a professional learning culture, one that values continuous learning throughout the organization.

The NTC has 200 staff members working across the United States. By holding to a growth mindset, it became one of the best nonprofits in the country. The center is highly sought after by both clients and employers. Early research on the effect of the NTC's instructionally focused and well-implemented mentoring program has revealed that new teachers want to stay in the classroom longer and are better at instructing the most underserved students. Veteran teachers who serve as mentors continuously learn in communities of practice (personal communication, April 15, 2015).

New Teacher Induction Program, Montgomery County Schools, Maryland

In addition to the nationwide approach carved out by the New Teacher Center, a number of state, county, and local new teacher programs were created. All are designed to provide new teachers the support they require in order to apply their university learning to their classrooms and to become members of vibrant learning communities. Gail Epps, program manager of the New Teacher Induction program of the Montgomery County Public Schools (MCPS), reports that the program supports and retains novice, experienced (but new to the district), and substitute teachers. The goals include: (1) improving instructional practice and (2) developing the leadership capacity of new-to-MCPS educators, mentors, and other critical personnel. The MCPS program has established strategic processes for operational excellence, customer service, and shared accountability. Professional learning activities focus on school improvement and student achievement. New teachers are expected to teach creative problem-solving skills and foster social–emotional learning, incorporate new assessment practices, create a positive classroom environment, and design lessons. These new teachers consider peer mentoring a significant part of their induction program.

The mentors are supported and guided to focus on strategies, practices, activities, and assessments needed to be an effective mentor. Through an ambitious agenda, mentors become better teachers, better mentors, and better leaders. Epps said they plan to expand the program to include the practice of whole-staff reflective strategies and to implement equitable practices across the system, providing cultural knowledge and adapting to diversity. The program has established a learning culture that invites risk-taking, creates diversity, and builds a strong sense of efficacy (personal communication, May 13, 2015).

Center for Teaching and Learning, Edgecomb, Maine

Nancie Atwell, awarded the Global Teacher prize in 2015 by the Varkey Foundation, is now known as the World's Best Teacher ('World's best teacher,' 2015). Atwell understands participatory, generative teaching and learning, and possesses an entrepreneurial spirit. In order to experiment with and refine a philosophy of teaching and learning, she built a demonstration K–8 local school, known as the Center for Teaching and Learning, based on encouraging learners' interests as a major part of curriculum and instruction. Students are invested in their learning because they choose how they are going to learn. Students assess their own work through interactions with other students and with teachers. There are no quizzes or tests. Within a traditional skills framework, students have choices about topics and how they will design their learning. The center invites public and private teachers from around the world to learn from Atwell's new approaches and explore her philosophy. Educators choose to come to this center because they are interested in her enterprise and it piques their own interests. They choose what they will take away for experimentation in their own classrooms, leaving behind the parts of Atwell's philosophy they feel will not work for them.

Teacher Leadership Academy, Grand Rapids, Michigan

Seeking to be "innovative, not just responsive" motivated Kent Intermediate School District (ISD) in Grand Rapids, Michigan, to develop a Teacher Leadership Academy. Marcia Logie, academy facilitator, described the purpose as "to grow teachers with the knowledge, skills, and attitudes that enable them to lead and influence others within and beyond the classroom." In partnership with Grand Valley University, the Kent ISD established the academy to assist teachers in securing an advanced teacher preparation certification or credits toward a master's in educational leadership after 18 months of courses and practice. While enrolled in the academy and after graduation, participant teachers accept various leadership roles in the district, such as coach, mentor, instructional specialist, and committee chair. Teachers who participate learn knowledge and skills needed to be successful leaders in their schools, to improve their own instruction, and to collaborate with colleagues. Teacher leaders become contributing members of learning communities.

Many teachers involved in the academy testify that their experiences transformed their teaching practice and work with their colleagues. Consider one such testimonial by a teacher who completed the academy:

> I wanted to learn more so that I could help other teachers. I wanted to be a voice. I wanted to be a mentor. So I read and absorbed as much as I could from every powerful book that was placed into my hand and from the work and activities that advanced our vision. I have offered my services for mentoring, coaching, and supporting my colleagues. I am no longer in my shell. (Personal communication, May 23, 2015)

Values-Based Leadership, Denver Public Schools, Colorado

"Don't wait, lead!" is a simple yet profound message created by the Denver superintendent, Tom Boasberg. These three words served as a touchstone and helped promote an innovative and entrepreneurial spirit throughout the Denver Public Schools (DPS). According to Nikki Rivera, a director of the Culture, Equity, and Leadership Team (CELT), "A strong and intentional culture is the lifeblood of an organization, and a healthy school culture is the 'secret sauce' that allows improvement strategies to thrive and flourish" (personal communication, June 10, 2015). In 2011, DPS embarked on a journey to become a values-based organization. In partnership with DaVita, a Denver-based health care provider, DPS established the CELT (similar to DaVita's internal Wisdom team) as well as a portfolio of values-based leadership learning and development opportunities for all 14,000-plus Denver educators.

In DPS everyone is considered an educator. Educators from across the district participate in values-based leadership opportunities that promote reflection, inquiry, dialogue, and a sense of oneness. The district believes leadership is more about disposition than position, and this belief is reflected in a number of new and innovative programs:

- Denver Teacher Residency—launched in 2009—was the first district-operated teacher residency program in the nation (www.denverteacherresidency.org).
- Teacher leadership—launched in 2010. By 2017 every district school will have at least two team leads (i.e., teacher leaders) who serve in the classroom for half a day and then observe, coach, and lead professional learning and provide feedback to colleagues. Team leads are part of the school's leadership team and work alongside the principal and assistant principal (teacherleader.dpsk12.org).
- Culture, Equity, and Leadership Team—launched in 2011—is the first district-operated organizational and development department in the nation (celt.dpsk12.org/).
- Personalized learning for students and staff—launched 2011 (imaginarium.dpsk12.org).
- Design Thinking Lab—launched in 2014—is open to anyone in the district who wants to use a human-centered approach beginning with the end user in mind and helps to achieve innovative and creative solutions to complex problems (imaginarium.dpsk12.org/).

Rivera reports that the commitment to creating a values-based culture throughout DPS is creating a shift to broad-based, skillful leadership. Schools are creating strong and intentional school cultures, implementing school improvement strategies, and steadily making academic gains. According to an annual engagement survey (CollaboRATE), overall engagement scores have increased steadily, with team leads among the highest scorers in the district. All positive indicators, says Rivera, as the Denver Public Schools strive to meet their vision: Every child succeeds! (personal communication, June 10, 2015).

Innovative Lab Network, United States

A network of states was organized in 2010 to produce models of learning designs informed by the shared work of states, districts, and schools. By 2015, 10 states had joined the network, supported by the Council of Chief State Officers. This network's purpose was to design a new education system that improves deeper learning outcomes for all students, without increased funding. "Deep learning" refers to a core consensus of what is needed now and in the future, elevating self-direction, collective inquiry, and both formal and informal learning into a "pedagogy of emergence."

Innovative Lab Network (ILN) is an example of frameworks being used within and across states that are "adaptive, organic, and employ higher order efforts to transform education systems" (González, 2014b, p. 7). They co-design and deploy resources differently in order to define learning outcomes, create conditions for emergent innovation, and share practices that facilitate systemic design efforts.

Wisconsin created a Regional Lab to focus on personalized professional development for educators. Kentucky authorized the creation of Districts of Innovation, giving districts additional flexibility to pursue innovative and adaptive practices. In both cases, ILN membership enabled the design of solutions appropriate to local problems and interests. Five other state labs have created professional development systems for deeper learning. Each lab attends to developing new bottom-up cultures that encourage risk-taking embedded in the dailiness of work, while protecting these systems from narrow policy-focused, compliance mindsets (González, 2014).

CONCLUSION

The stories told in this chapter illustrate the principles of professional learning in high capacity learning cultures. These designs address issues unique to the organization's needs and interests, yet universal in substance. A broad range of collaborative structures was created to support goals while provoking innovation and continuous improvement.

Several of the learning organizations reveal how designs become embedded in a holding community environment (Manitoba, Maplewood Richmond Heights, Center for Teaching and Learning in Maine, and Denver). In other stories, designs dissolve boundaries and reach wider audiences (New Teacher Center, Ohio Voices Montgomery County Public Schools, Tomorrow Makers library project, and Innovative Lab Network). Still others are designed for a specific district or school (Denver Leadership Academy, Kent Intermediate's Teacher Leadership Academy, and Hillbrook School). These designs engage the reciprocal processes central to leadership capacity.

The pursuit of leadership capacity asks that organizations and professionals rethink professional learning in order to create transformative changes in patterns of relationships, assumptions, and mindsets. Optimism points to an expanding national and international focus on design thinking, realigned governance, and teacher leadership. The confluence and technological sophistication now available have triggered an eagerness to share ideas, designs, prototypes, models, and promising practices. In the following chapters, the learning and leading skills introduced in this chapter are described in more depth. The following chapter describes specific strategies and protocols for creating robust communities, conversations, and inquiries. Chapter 5 delves deeply into the journey to access, apply, and construct knowledge.

QUESTIONS FOR PERSONAL REFLECTION

1. Review Figure 3.1. In your school or organization, which principles are in place? Which may serve as next steps in deepening your professional learning culture?
2. In Kegan's theory of development, different levels are described. One or two may resonate with you. What level(s) describe where you see yourself? You may be in transition or situated in more than one level, as these often vary with context. Design two steps in a professional learning path to move your development forward.

QUESTIONS FOR GROUP REFLECTION

1. Select one of the questions below, or generate one of your own, for conversation.
   - How will your team simultaneously attend to the interests of students and meet state or district mandates?
   - What leadership processes described in this chapter could assist your school or organization to create a more collaborative professional learning culture?
   - How might your team create platforms that allow great ideas generated on the local level to be shared across the country?
2. Gather a group of colleagues interested in design thinking. Consult the Internet and explore resources for designs (e.g., REDlab at Stanford University: web.stanford.edu/group/redlab/cgi-bin/index. php; www.edutopia.org; www.designthinkingforeducators.com; Designthinkinginschools.org; www.gettingsmart.com; ideo.com). Is there a preferred approach best fitted to your situation? What criteria did you use for selection?
3. In Chapter 2 you assessed the leadership capacity of your school based on Figure 2.1. Consider Figure 3.2 in this chapter. Select and discuss your three next steps with two or three colleagues.

CHAPTER 4

Collaborative Dimensions of Leadership

Collaborative leadership communities do not happen by chance; they take hard work, dedication, and commitment to shared values. Participants in high leadership capacity schools understand that skill building is on a dual track: how to teach and how to lead, mirror images of each other. In the previous chapter, we described the importance of moving professional learning from an event-based model to an inquiry-focused model, based on design thinking, which shapes new cultures of leadership. Further, we acknowledged the role of Every Student Succeeds in redefining professional learning as it relates to sustained capacity building. In this chapter, communication skills are advanced as the reciprocal processes of deep learning essential for fostering leadership capacity.

Initially, when the Oak Valley Middle School leadership team began to explore professional learning communities as a way to build capacity, it floundered. While teachers supported the idea of being more in control of their own meetings and professional learning, conflicts ensued. Teachers complained that meetings went on too long and were not focused, and some voices dominated. After reading about professional learning communities in the work of DuFour and Eaker (1998), one staff member introduced the team to four critical questions: (1) What do we expect students to learn? (2) How will we know they are learning? (3) How will we respond if they do not learn? and (4) How will we respond if they already know it?

These four questions provided short-term focus to the work at Oak Valley, but debates over student outcomes stalled progress. It was not until the staff developed their own working agreements and established a collaborative compact (Garmston & Zimmerman, 2013a) that they began to listen and talk to one another in ways leading toward self-organization. Another breakthrough came when they began to explore protocol designs, which outlined procedures for facilitating groupwork and structuring conversations.

LEADERSHIP COMMUNITIES

In Chapter 3, two forms of learning communities are described: professional learning communities and communities of practice. They both have the potential to create social systems supported by the web of relationships in which learning is grounded in the types of conversations proposed in this chapter.

Leadership suggests that community members learn from one another by developing positive reciprocal patterns of relationships. Such patterns emerge when participants linger in conversation long enough to deepen understandings and work through conflicting viewpoints. Indeed, this is a critical test for all communities: knowing how to embrace and work with differences. High leadership capacity suggests a strong commitment by all to develop communication skills to foster inquiry, reflection, and divergent thinking. Slowing the conversations by applying the collaborative dimensions of leadership outlined in this chapter expands capacity for authentic inquiry and reflection—essential cornerstones of leadership communities. In leadership communities, participants take responsibility for ensuring that their work increases the capacity of the group.

When the Oak Valley staff members began to talk about their differences, they realized that while many teachers held different viewpoints, these viewpoints were not so far apart. As Juanita observed, "We were really smart alone, but could not figure out how to work smart together. We were polarized; it wasn't until we realized how to bring all voices into the conversation that our work together changed." At this point in their journey, they were ready to learn more about the collaborative dimensions of leadership.

FOUR COLLABORATIVE DIMENSIONS OF LEADERSHIP CAPACITY

Four collaborative dimensions of leadership have particular promise for enhancing capacity by provoking self-organization. While some groups may function well without conscious attention to these collaborative dimensions, more find that by learning these skills they strengthen the collective capacity for leading. These four dimensions are: (1) structuring efficient protocols for participation; (2) setting standards and working agreements for collaboration; (3) embedding the linguistics for listening into conversations; and (4) facilitating conversational flows. These four learning contexts are summarized in Figure 4.1.

Figure 4.1. The Four Dimensions of Collaboration

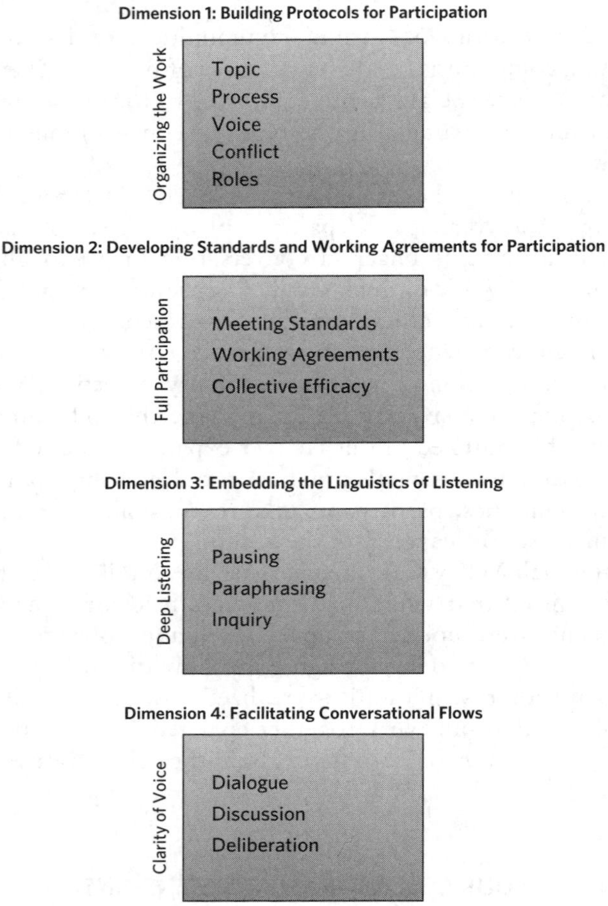

Dimension 1: Building Protocols for Participation

Organizing the Work

Topic
Process
Voice
Conflict
Roles

Dimension 2: Developing Standards and Working Agreements for Participation

Full Participation

Meeting Standards
Working Agreements
Collective Efficacy

Dimension 3: Embedding the Linguistics of Listening

Deep Listening

Pausing
Paraphrasing
Inquiry

Dimension 4: Facilitating Conversational Flows

Clarity of Voice

Dialogue
Discussion
Deliberation

Skilled learning communities are efficient at organizing their work, expect full participation and deep listening, and celebrate group insights. In some communities, these abilities seem to emerge spontaneously without much guidance, while others struggle and require additional working agreements to find success. To start the processes of successful collaboration, communities can benefit from self-evaluation in order to identify a focus. For some groups, starting with working agreements can be most productive. For others, who have little experience with learning communities, and are leader-dependent, a protocol can introduce and model the power of generative learning in community. "Generative" means that a group has the capacity to self-organize for learning to create collective knowledge and action. Figure 4.2 can help determine where best to begin.

Any community can benefit from learning more about the four collaborative dimensions. Together, these dimensions create the conditions for optimal learning and produce leadership communities that self-organize to build leadership capacity. These approaches create networks of practice that enable a community to resolve conflicts, discover shared beliefs, and design effective ways of working together. A cultural shift is the result, enabling community members to say, "We are a generative learning community; we are increasing our leadership capacity and moving toward a robust understanding of effective teaching and learning."

Figure 4.2. Diagnosing Starting Places for the Collaborative Dimensions of Leadership

Problem	Starting Place
Ways to Organize Work Sessions	
Concerns about wasting time, lack of closure, and conflicts. Work in groups is discouraging. Little experience with effective facilitation.	Participants seek out protocols: online, from a neighboring school, or other workshops. Members of the leadership team serve as the guides. (See Building Protocols for Participation, p. 68)
Full Participation	
Group members do not feel safe and do not trust that the ways the group works together will support their learning. A few do all the talking.	Review and adopt meeting standards. Collaboratively work to develop working agreements and work toward the adoption of a collaborative compact. (See Standards and Working Agreements Build Trust, p. 68)
Deep Listening	
Discussions feel rushed and are confusing, and the conversation is often diverted. Sometimes the appointed leader fills the void with talk. Group members do not feel heard.	Before each meeting, set aside time for the group to study the skills of "deep listening." Practice these skills during the meeting and evaluate impact at the end of the meeting. (See Embedded Linguistics of Listening, p. 73)
Clarity of Voice	
Working agreements are in place, but participants still feel that individuals are not listening to one another. Time management continues to be a problem, and some complain about too much talk time.	Study the types of conversations below. Identify contexts in which each of these conversations would be helpful and commit this to an action plan on paper. For most groups, this dimension is best studied last. (See Facilitating Conversational Flows, p. 79)

BUILDING PROTOCOLS FOR PARTICIPATION

Design thinking is an umbrella construct from which participants can create their own protocols. It is not necessarily a methodology with prescribed steps, but rather a process guided by fundamental principles. For example, in the "discovery phase" of design thinking, a team might make choices about how to define the challenge or how to conduct needed research. In high capacity schools, design principles shape ways of working, allowing for flexibility and fluidity.

Protocols describe participatory design structures that empower educators to create meaningful learning experiences without extensive knowledge of organizational development. That is, they provide structures for substantive work while also building trust and communication skills. A benefit of a protocol is that it provides a written plan for facilitation, allowing the group to work without an appointed leader. The National School Reform Faculty (NSRF, 2014) and the School Reform Initiative (2016) have more than 110 protocols on their websites. The NSRF (2014) has set a mission to create and disseminate protocols that allow educators to "collaborate effectively in democratic communities that foster educational equity and social justice."

Pomerantz and Ippolito (2015) found that the use of protocols expands teacher capacity for leadership. These researchers introduced a group of reading specialists to a *collaborative assessment protocol*. After experiencing these protocol-based discussions, the specialists identified the following benefits: mutual respect, highly focused and productive conversations, and validation from colleagues for their ideas. Initially they found it important to follow the protocols as they were designed. They concluded, however, that real capacity building came when the protocols were collaboratively adapted to meet the needs of local groups. Further, they reported that practice with these protocols in job-alike learning communities built their confidence, while enabling them to apply and adapt protocols for work in their school settings.

Initially, protocols may stipulate specific sequences of activities and feel artificial. Yet, well-designed protocols are purposeful and meet the five essential meeting standards identified by Doyle and Straus (1976): focusing on one topic, focusing on one process at a time, balancing participation, allowing for diverse viewpoints, and specifying roles.

STANDARDS AND WORKING AGREEMENTS BUILD TRUST

In many schools, meeting standards and working agreements have been optional. When collaborative work goes smoothly, these agreements do not seem necessary; but these commitments can prove essential in times of conflict.

Breakdowns in trust caused by conflict can distort communication processes and render collaboration difficult, if not impossible. When participants do not speak their truth, it remains hidden. Consider two stories from the field. In a moment of truth, a 15-year veteran teacher told one of us, "When I first started teaching, I tried to talk in staff meetings, but no one listened. So that is why I never talk in a staff meeting." A colleague and veteran middle and high school principal, Bill Sommers, described how difficult it can be to get teachers to share their excellence: "When I ask teachers to share their knowledge, they often respond that because of a fear of reprisals they do not want to be singled out" (personal communication, July 2013). These are not isolated instances. Establishing standards and working agreements helps to foster consistency, trust, and the capacity for communities to grow and learn together.

Without opportunities to delve into the deepest thinking of group members, collaborative work stays at the surface and focus remains superficial. Most educators can articulate what they aspire to in their work, but without mutual trust, collective success remains elusive. Unless group members feel safe and free from judgments, they are not likely to speak personal truths. In her dissertation, Westsmith (2014) studied relational trust in her school as defined by Louis (2007) and concluded that relational trust was an essential attribute of high capacity schools.

Forsyth, Adams, and Hoy (2011) define collective trust as the reciprocal relationships enhancing collective trust—a belief in the mutual benefits of collaboration. Over the course of 30 years they identified collective trust as an essential ingredient in school reform. They suggest that designs for learning that support reciprocal interactions encourage the open exchange of ideas. By consistently applying meeting standards and working agreements, communities build collective trust over time, and their conversations begin to probe the depths of each member's thinking, increasing the capacity to learn and lead in community.

Universal Meeting Standards

In *How to Make Meetings Work,* Doyle and Straus (1976) explored the question: What is the minimum number of meeting standards needed for effective meetings? Garmston (2012) adapted this seminal work to identify five meeting standards that have passed the test of time. These standards are understood as *universal* meeting standards because they satisfy basic human needs to understand and make meaning from experience. The five universal meeting standards are the following:

1. Focus on One Topic at a Time. Undertaking one topic at a time helps to initiate and sustain focus by satisfying the need for understanding and clarity. Therefore, it is an essential conversational tool. Even a 1st-grader can plead for focus by reminding a peer, "I was talking about owls, not dinosaurs." Researchers have identified attentional processes, those systems that both select and sustain focal processing, as essential for learning (Sylwester & Cho, 1992/1993). Hence, the framing of one topic at a time assists the brain in focusing and sustaining attention. When this standard is in place, participants redirect sidetracked conversations in much the same way as the young child described above.

2. Apply One Process at a Time. Often groups mix up processes. For example, in the classic protocol for brainstorming, some participants limit creativity by prematurely changing the processes from "accepting all ideas without critique" to "judging each idea as it arises." When a group understands the expectations for one process at a time, such as with the brainstorming protocol, any member can redirect the group. For example, a participant might say, "That idea was just criticized. Let's stick to nonjudgmental brainstorming."

When building agendas, it is helpful to pair a verb (process) with the topic. Consider these differences: (1) brainstorm options for "homework club"; (2) discuss "homework club" options; (3) decide how to implement the "homework club." Each one of these items sets a different expectation, from considering options to deciding, therefore evoking different neural patterns. Brain researchers from the Queensland Brain Institute (2014) have found that thinking about action primes the brain nearly 2 seconds before the activation of voluntary movement. Therefore, clear processes prime the brain for effective action.

3. Balance Participation and Keep Meetings Interactive. Working agreements, described later in this chapter, bring specificity to this standard. Each community has unique interpretations of how to balance participation. For example, one group might decide to pause for a check-in to allow those who have not spoken to do so. Another group might establish a job, such as "process checker," in which one participant collects data and reports back to the group by saying something like, "So far five people have had a chance to speak. Who else wants to speak on this subject?" Despite these refinements, some groups find participation is still not balanced. At this point, the group needs to examine what is occurring under the surface and ask whether it could be based on a history of low trust.

For cultures with a long history of judgment and criticism, it can be helpful to use a protocol that alternates between small- and large-group discussions, such as "Think, Pair, Share." Most participants speak in a small group, and when colleagues encourage them, will speak up in a larger meeting. Shifting between small- and whole-group interactions is an effective way to balance participation.

When participants have opportunities to speak early in the process, it creates a readiness for speaking later as well, thus bringing all voices into the room. Bob Chadwick (2013), a forest ranger turned conflict resolution expert, designed an opening ritual for priming participation called "grounding." In a grounding, everyone is asked to make a statement about what he or she is thinking or feeling about an issue, thus providing each a chance to speak, feel heard, and feel acknowledged. Such opportunities to interact constitute a great gift to the human psyche, for oxytocin is activated by human interactions. When this opening occurs in the networks of the prefrontal cortex of the brain, it further increases the ability to trust and think together (Glaser, 2014).

4. Use Conflicts Productively. Conflicts left unresolved produce high stress in communities and tend to literally create dis-ease. One of the major causes of stress is lack of trust, in which the neurotransmitter cortisol floods the brain, shutting down executive functions needed to manage the brain's higher cortical functions. With this emotional response, humans revert to preferred default behaviors: fight (argue the point), flight (take easiest way out), freeze (disengage from the meeting and sit it out), or appease (show agreement to avoid attack). Judith Glaser (2014) notes that disagreements often block honest and productive sharing of knowledge.

This meeting standard can be clarified through the development of collaborative working agreements. For example, working agreements for using conflict productively might be stated as follows:

- Summarize the conflicting viewpoints
- Challenge ideas not people
- Give labels to "hot buttons"
- Agree to disagree

By providing language and processes with which to work through conflicts, participants are able to slow down, take breaths, and think more carefully about what is important. Agreement is not mandatory, and occasionally the best course of action is to agree to disagree and move on.

Often conflicts arise from small misunderstandings. For example, using a protocol designed on the principles of interest-based bargaining, Zimmerman brought key teacher leaders together to work through a seemingly intractable problem: Each of the five schools in the district had a different grading cycle, making it difficult to coordinate work on standards and assessment. Fifteen minutes into the meeting, after sorting out the various "interests" of the participants, the teachers realized that each school had held a different definition of "midterm" reporting. Once the definition was cleared up, the conflict was resolved. Later, a teacher said, "I was ready for World War III. I was so surprised it was just a misunderstanding about the timetable for midterm reports. That was the sticking point." What appeared intractable had a simple solution that became evident by working through the conflict.

5. Share Responsibility for Meeting Roles. In the 1970s, as meeting management became a "science," consultants encouraged the clear delineation of roles by separating the appointed leader from the role of facilitator, assigning a recorder to capture ideas, and appointing a timekeeper. These roles were singular, and those appointed often became *de facto* leaders of the group, with others remaining passive. This can be particularly sensitive for women, who more often than not were given the role of scribe. To avoid these traps, the responsibility for roles needs to be shared and rotated.

Garmston (2012) argues that the success of a group is derived from informed participation rather than specific roles, knowledge, or skills. This observation suggests that participants take equitable responsibility and rotate designated roles. Hence, the most important role in a leadership community is that of engaged participant. In taking responsibility for engagement, it is incumbent on each person to pay attention to personal, subgroup, and whole-group engagement. For example, when personal engagement wanes, a leadership action might be to pay attention to the rest of the group and intervene with a process check such as, "I think we may be repeating ourselves; are we ready to summarize the important points?"

When these five standards are met, participants trust the processes and are more ready to attend fully to the tasks at hand. The universal meeting standards above set the foundation for the development and refinement of working agreements.

Working Agreements

For teachers, time is an especially valuable asset; hence the effective management of meetings becomes an essential leadership act. When group members are asked what is important for successful collaboration, they often suggest similar goals: to feel safe, to be heard, and to be productive. These needs form the foundation for an expanded list of desired group behaviors, defined as working agreements. In general, working agreements should be stated as positive intentions. For example, if a desired behavior is stated in the negative, such as "no interrupting," the group changes it to the positive, "only one voice at a time."

The key to the success and sustainability of working agreements is evaluation cycles in which the group reflects on how well agreements have been kept. Focusing on one or two working agreements per meeting is an efficient way to accomplish this end. Initially, an anonymously written 1–10 ranking produces the most honest responses, which are then shared publicly.

As groups mature, open conversations about the successful use of working agreements set the stage for direct feedback substantiated by behavioral evidence. When groups skip this critical evaluation step, agreements begin to erode. In contrast, when groups become aware of obstacles to effective work, group members change their response patterns and subsequently transform their culture, creating leadership communities in which all are responsible for shared success. Ideally these agreements are a living document to be reviewed regularly and when internalized influence interactions with both colleagues and students.

In *Lemons to Lemonade,* Garmston and Zimmerman (2013b) suggest the use of a *collaborative compact,* which is a protocol designed to assist communities to self-organize for productive learning. The primary premise of this compact is that each person is an essential participant; hence, participants need to be responsible for monitoring their own and one another's behavior (for more on this concept, see learningforward.org/docs/default-source/jsd-april-2013/garmston342.pdf).

EMBEDDED LINGUISTICS OF LISTENING

Many conversations are characterized by a form of autobiographical listening in which each person adds to the conversation based primarily on personal frames of reference. Often, these conversations are in small groups and relate to topics introduced by the group members. When narrow personal perspectives limit larger group conversations, the conversations can unravel into subgroups. When participants spend more time thinking about their next comments, it can be said "they listen with one ear."

Deep Listening

To avoid the pitfalls wrought by abbreviated attentiveness, learning communities benefit by adopting specific linguistic tools that foster deep listening. The judicious use of pausing, paraphrasing, and inquiry through questioning can expand the conversation by opening up space for listening, reflection, and dialogue.

Pausing. For the purist, the pause may not be considered a linguistic convention. However, the pause gives speech its cadence and shape; it provides microseconds for thinking; it signals a respect for others. The pause allows group members to move in sync with one another by signaling turn taking, or the need to stop and think. The pause is a respectful way to be with others by affording the time for each member to move beyond personal thoughts and fully absorb what another is saying.

In *Seven Thousand Ways to Listen,* Mark Nepo (2012) wondered: If there are 7,000 different languages and ways of speaking, there must be at least 7,000 ways to listen. He reflected, "To *enter* deep listening, I have had to learn ways of emptying and opening; how to keep beginning. I've had to lean into all that I don't understand, accepting that I am changed by what I hear" (p. xi, emphasis in original). When the listener pauses and lingers so as to truly hear and understand the other, the power of listening can be understood as a leadership act.

The pause allows time for small reflections, a necessary ingredient in the continuous development of individual and organizational learning capacities. Any teacher who has used Mary Budd Rowe's (1986) strategy of "wait time" knows how important the pause can be to support thinking. For teaching, coaching, facilitating, and consulting, pauses give time to check the response of the listener, helping the speaker know how to pace the conversation by allowing a moment for thought, or to let the other person speak.

Metacognition, or the ability to think about thinking, increases with quiet reflection time. It can be helpful to build in community routines for silent reflection in order to foster metacognition. Parker Palmer (1998) in *The Courage to Teach* emphasizes that solitude within community invites time for reflecting and absorbing information in a way that maintains the integrity of each person's inner self.

The pause opens up choices for the group; it gives a chance to check in with one another, to think about the quality of the interactions, and to forecast options for responding. When pausing to reflect on others' words, the group begins to listen in synchrony as they become immersed in a leadership culture.

Paraphrasing. While pausing may be overlooked as a linguistic skill, paraphrasing is more often underutilized. Native speakers of a language may navigate conversations without much thought about how they come to understand the meaning or intention behind the words. The listener's role may appear passive, perhaps using head nods or sub-vocalizations to indicate agreement, or a frown for confusion or disagreement. Conversations ebb and flow, either moving the conversation forward or changing course by introducing a new topic.

Conversations in leadership communities, however, require intentional processes for listening deeply and reflecting back what is understood. Reciprocal processes, such as the paraphrase, expand the capacity of the group to learn from and build on one another's thinking. A paraphrase is never an exact repeat; instead, the words are filtered through another's linguistic system and then restated in a way that makes sense. A paraphrase is the listener's affirmation of understanding. So the first rule of paraphrasing is for the listener to say what he or she understands the speaker to be saying. This productive back-and-forth communication—the judicious use of paraphrasing—can clear up any misunderstandings.

To craft a paraphrase, one focuses on the ambiguous parts of the message. Nouns and verbs convey meaning, and yet they can be interpreted differently. For example, in a meeting about standards-based report cards, a friend reported that through skillful paraphrases the group discovered subtle but different interpretations of "grades." Some teachers based grades on effort and others on scores. Afterward, the teacher commented, "It was as if the paraphrase was used to hang important ideas on a clothesline and then we could look at the ideas."

Like the pause, the paraphrase serves to open up the conversation and provoke a more contemplative way of working. When something is restated in another way, group members hear it differently, making meanings more nuanced and robust. What is less obvious, but even more important, is that when the paraphrase is used in leadership communities, it enhances the group's ability to think more deeply. It mediates thinking by bringing clarity, linking ideas, and opening up abstractions in ways that make them more understandable.

All paraphrases have the potential to distort as well as clarify meaning. If not carefully crafted, they can be manipulative by valuing some ideas over others. For example, an art program, Visual Thinking Strategies, uses paraphrasing as a key pedagogical strategy (Yenawine, 2013). In this program, rather than telling children and adults about art, the teacher uses paraphrasing to encourage the participants to keep talking and to leave space for the learners to figure out the meaning on their own. The teacher's role is to paraphrase what the participants say by reflecting the words back and linking key ideas, but not inserting teacher ideas. Yenawine found that if teachers were not careful, teacher bias often seeped into the paraphrase; and so in the initial stages, he asked teachers to focus only on accurate paraphrasing. In addition, the teachers grew to understand that when they paraphrased some students' comments in greater detail—and others not as much—they were demonstrating a bias for the ideas and privileging some voices over the others. The teachers who used the program for several years became elegant with paraphrasing and reported that the process changed the way they thought of classroom conversations.

Paraphrasing is a gift of listening and a powerful linguistic tool that enhances shared cognition. It signals appreciation for another's words, thoughts, and ideas. When groups expand collective understanding by linking ideas, they not only summarize, but also amplify the capacity of the learning community.

Inquiry. Teachers naturally use questions to check for student understanding and extend conversations in the classroom; they also use taxonomies of questions to increase thoughtful, high-level responses. In some classrooms, teachers shift the locus of responsibility to the students, and the students ask their own questions about what they want to learn. In project-based learning, students work together to solve open-ended problems. The focus is on thinking strategies and knowledge domains. The goal is to help students develop flexible knowledge, collaboration, and self-direction by asking what they know, need to know, and how to access the information required to solve the problem. In such classrooms, a culture of inquiry exists in which students view learning as a process of asking questions about things they do not know and about things that emerge out of what they are coming to know.

In adult learning communities also, a culture of inquiry creates a collective mindset in which participants become leaders of their own learning. Instead of merely accepting mandates, teachers ask questions about assumptions and generalizations. They explore understandings, perceptions, interpretations, and intentions. They review the supporting research or references and seek opportunities for adaptation.

Likewise, teachers can ask questions about the craft of teaching and about their schools and communities, creating their own action research by seeking answers to puzzles that emerge from classroom practice. Instead of producing correct answers, the questions in cultures of inquiry open up paths for exploration and create more questions than answers.

The most thought-provoking questions, for adults and students alike, occur as collective thinking in collaborative environments—questions that emerge spontaneously from collective thought. Teachers begin to ask school-wide questions: Which clusters of students are not doing well? How will we expand parent involvement? What other schools in the district might we form networks with? What evidence do we have that the vision is becoming manifest throughout the school? These are fertile questions for inquiry.

Questions deepen intellectual curiosity. The most powerful questions cause shifts in cognition or what cognitive coaches (Costa & Garmston, 2015) call *cognitive shifts*. In *The Constructivist Leader* (Lambert et al., 1995), the authors referred to such shifts as "breaking set with old assumptions" (pp. 36–37). This view of inquiry as an interactive process invites deep reflection and an awareness of how the group is changing its mind and breaking away from outdated assumptions.

Informal action research has long been seen as a vital approach for breaking set with old assumptions. In Chapter 3, the story of a high school in northern Alberta, Canada, presented an example of a school nurturing a culture of inquiry. In such cultures, educators often ask questions and seek answers through extended action research. In the most formal application of action research, educators explore a research question and data are triangulated; for example, tests scores might be paired with examples from student work and from teacher records.

The power of the question is dependent not only on its linguistic structure, but also on the proactive ways participants support thinking. When the question is paired with pausing and paraphrasing, the pace of the conversation allows other questions to emerge from spaces in the conversation.

In true cultures of inquiry, nothing is sacred. For example, in the current iteration of standards, there has been strong emphasis on nonfiction reading and writing, the explanation being that nonfiction (essay) reading and writing make students "college ready." A conversation at Oak Valley Middle School illustrates how an inquiring stance can turn into a form of action research, a systematic inquiry into questions of practice. The teachers' concern regarding an overemphasis on nonfiction texts led them to a collective inquiry into the origin of this focus. During a moment of frustration, Wayne burst out, "What is the reasoning behind this rule on nonfiction? We need clarity before we can proceed." Joan replied, "Let's see what we can find out."

To get started, the Oak Valley staff generated a list of questions, and then each teacher chose two questions to research before the next meeting. When the staff reconvened 2 weeks later, everyone had something to report; the air bustled with energy like a class excited about learning something new. Raul was excited to share that the focus of the Common Core State Standards on "informational texts" was for reading and not for writing. He read with emphasis, "Listen to this: In 4th grade, students should read a balance of 50% literary and 50% informational texts. By 8th grade the split skews slightly to 45/55% in favor of informational. This gives the English department a lot of leeway." Joan interjected, "I, too, found something I didn't know." With all eyes on Joan, she went on to explain: "It turns out the standards were mapped on the National Assessment for Educational Progress assessment for writing. By 8th grade, students are expected to spend 30% of their time conveying experience, 35% explaining, and 35% persuading. What is important is not that the students write nonfiction, but that they have a chance to explore genres to learn how to express their ideas." She added with emphasis, "Now that is a worthy focus for my 8th-grade English class." More teachers contributed what they had learned as well. By questioning the standards, the Oak Valley teachers were now emboldened to make reasonable adaptations. As Joan admitted, "This process of questioning the standards brings me hope; I can use what I already know and apply the standards to develop refinements."

For Oak Valley teachers, "doubt" was a powerful ally, as it was this doubt that challenged them to critically question and assess the integrity of what they were being asked to do. Snow-Gerono (2005) found that when teachers support one another in community and begin to explore uncertainty, they move toward cultures of inquiry, exploring the edges of what is known and not known. In fact, compelling unanswered questions tend to stay in the mind until satisfactory answers are found. The importance of collective inquiry in building deep understandings about practice cannot be overemphasized.

Benefits of Collective Inquiry

When groups work well together, they can experience a special quality identified by Mihaly Csikszentmihalyi (2008) as "flow," in which participants find themselves immersed in conversations that are energizing and have a high degree of focus and a sense of timelessness. Csikszentmihalyi describes flow as the harnessing of positive emotions in the service of learning. For some, it is the ultimate experience of learning. This explains why sometimes meetings leave participants energized and excited, while others are draining.

The leadership act of using inquiry to shape learning moves a learning community forward and harnesses the power of positive emotion and intentions. When participants are able to use pausing, paraphrasing, and inquiry together, they create a space for collective, generative constructivist learning, in which learning communities move toward increased knowledge about the craft of teaching, leadership, and learning. Being conscious of "how we are in conversation," while not necessarily in every context, is essential for leadership. These reciprocal relationships are highlighted in Figure 4.3.

When conversations work well, generative learning becomes dynamic, fluid, and emergent, instead of fragmented; these collective capacities inform leadership. An initial free flow of ideas coalesces into coherent understandings, forming networks of local knowledge. Furthermore, through conversation the internal knowledge of group members becomes public and hence serves as a resource. The ability to construct, sustain, and generate knowledge will be described in more detail in Chapter 5.

Figure 4.3. Generative Constructivist Learning

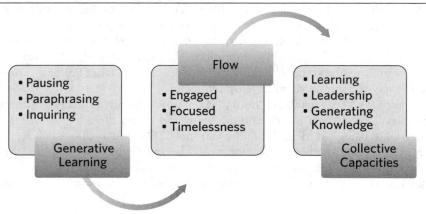

FACILITATING CONVERSATIONAL FLOWS

Conversations transmit the infinite unfolding of meaning that builds shared understandings and the social cognition that shapes culture. The derivation of the word *conversation*, from Latin, is "turning together." Conversation by definition is a reciprocal process; however, not all learning conversations are created equally. For most daily activities, speakers converse without giving it much thought; it is a natural part of daily lives. In conversations, groups agree to tacit ground rules for acceptable interactions designed to keep social agreements, including but not limited to degrees of politeness, divulgence, and emotion. Communities consensually validate topics, both acceptable and taboo; indeed, these kinds of conversations serve us well in most of our daily lives.

To engage in leadership, participants need to become conscious of the differences among conversation flows, specifically dialogue, discussion, and deliberation. Each one of these types of conversations brings out different voices and serves different purposes. Figure 4.4 compares and contrasts the outcomes of these three different types of conversations.

The Voice of Dialogue

The Brazilian educator and philosopher Paolo Freire, in his classic *Pedagogy of the Oppressed* (1993), originally published in 1970, identified dialogue as an essential ingredient for creating change: "Dialogue is the encounter between men, mediated by the world, in order to name the world" (p. 69). Freire's treatise had its foundations in philosophical discourse and social

Figure 4.4. Distinctions Among Dialogue, Discussion, and Deliberation

	Dialogue	Discussion	Deliberation
Judgment	Suspended	Natural response	Judgment required
Norm	Listening, inquiring	Talking	Deciding
Understanding	Cognitive and reflective	Social or topical	Decisional
Response behaviors	Contemplative	Quick response	Consensus or conciliation
Generates	Openness	Fragmentation	Closure
Interactions	Mutual	Determine status	Debate
Interactive stance	Speaking with	Talking to	Debating about
Focus	Insights	Differences	Conclusions

science research; his aim was to liberate the oppressed and amplify voices previously silenced. He advocated for a system where equality among participants was essential, a condition achieved through reciprocity. More than 40 years later, many teachers have less freedom to shape their profession; indeed, in some places, especially low-performing schools, mandates and pacing guides render them oppressed.

In London, David Bohm (1990, 1998) discussed with colleagues the profound questions raised by debates surrounding nuclear science. He found that patterns of deliberation in daily conversations often blocked deep contemplation about the issues. Without slowing down and working to build deep reflection, Bohm noted, it was difficult to raise consciousness about critical global issues. He, like many of his contemporaries, worried that postwar cultures would not develop further without shared meanings, the basis of all cultures. It is in the act of raising consciousness that leadership capacity is liberated.

As he worked with others, Bohm began to distinguish "dialogue" from "discussion" or "debate." The etymological roots of discussion, for instance, are the same as those of "percussion," meaning to break things up. In contrast, dialogue seeks to bring ideas together through deep listening, involving pausing and paraphrasing, examining assumptions, and asking open-ended questions.

Principles of Dialogue

Schein (1993) and Isaacs (1999) have established ground rules for dialogue, which are expanded and enumerated in Figure 4.5. By setting aside time for dialogue, groups can learn to build sufficient common ground and mutual trust, and speak honestly.

Schein (1993), in his seminal work on organizational learning, argued that dialogue is the root of effective group action. Like Bohm, he describes how dialogue moves beyond active listening to focus on our thinking processes, leading to an understanding of how perception and cognition are formed. "An important goal of dialogue," Schein insists, "is to enable the *group* to reach a higher level of consciousness and creativity through the

Figure 4.5. Principles of Dialogue

- Apply pausing and paraphrasing to slow the conversation
- Listen and observe others
- Suspend assumptions, leave judgments outside the dialogue
- Search and pose questions to get at underlying meanings
- Welcome differences and pose questions to understand
- Listen to your own inner voice and make that explicit

gradual creation of a shared set of meanings and a 'common' thinking process"(p. 30, emphasis in original).

Dialogue is a cornerstone for creating leadership capacity in that all voices must weigh in, and appointed leaders become just one of the many voices. In dialogue each step in the process folds back on itself, creating giant patterns of conversation in the process of making meaning. In Chapter 6 this process of "folding back on itself" is proposed as a fundamental aspect of systemic change.

The Default Voice—Discussion

Discussions are the day-to-day fabric of social understanding and learning. Accordingly, discussions are the conversational norm; without thinking about it, discussions happen. While discussions are often the glue holding conversations together, they also can build an illusion of understanding, since discussions emerge from each individual's personal voice creating a patchwork of ideas. It is easy to stay on the surface and assume all are in agreement. However, this assumption misses the point that no two people interpret the world of meaning in the same way.

While it is not necessary to offer a model for how to conduct a discussion, it is important for groups to become conscious of the patterns emerging when they are in an automatic mode. Groups with expertise in dialogue, or skills in pausing, paraphrasing, and inquiry, can easily bring those skills to bear in a discussion, helping to bring focus and deepen understandings.

As leadership communities develop and mature, they become more self-reflective about their patterns of conversation and more fluid in the ability to move among different types of conversations. When participants learn to interact on multiple levels, they develop their own personal, reflective check-ins by asking the questions: "How am I engaged in this discussion and how is this discussion fostering my capacity to learn?"

A leadership act, at this point, becomes one of contribution. When the topic is of interest, contribute; when attention wanes, check in by summarizing and inquiring about next steps. For example, a team member might state, "We have about 20 minutes left, and I hear three big ideas which are. . . . Are we ready to move to the next step?" This action demonstrates personal responsibility that also brings the focus and the control back to the group as a whole and allows the group to figure out its next steps.

The Voice of Assertion—Deliberation

Deliberation is the conversational flow often used to make a decision and come to closure, thereby informing future actions. The flow of this conversation is different from dialogue and discussion. In deliberation, because the participants are making choices, they become more assertive and often use an advocacy process that serves to bring focus and to reach a decision.

In the Oak Valley Middle School example above, the group had been in a discussion for 40 minutes about the CCSS and how the standards supported informational texts. Participants were starting to repeat ideas. Principal Aretha observed, "We have identified many key ideas about how we want to approach the use of text in our classrooms." She paused, scanned the group for responses, and added, "Are we ready to decide on some next steps?" One teacher walked to the easel, "I will write down the ideas. Please summarize them for me. As I write, check my words for accuracy." After 10 ideas had been listed, the scribe surveyed the group, "Does anyone have anything to add?" Raul suggested, "I see a relationship between some of these; let's combine a few. We only have about 10 minutes left in our meeting, so let's turn to a neighbor and see if we agree." After a few minutes, he asked, "What connections are we noting?" Raul drew arrows to make the links and monitored for head nods and agreement. Finally, Aretha suggested closure: "I want to be respectful of our time, so I'll ask the secretary to type this up, send out the ideas in an email for one more review. We can return to the topic at our next meeting."

When groups have worked well together and taken time to be clear about group understandings, the process of deliberation goes smoothly. However, there are situations requiring careful attention to the structure of deliberation. For information about how to structure a balance between inquiry and advocacy, see Garmston and Zimmerman (2013b). For more detail, Korgerus and Tschappeler, in *The Decision Book: 50 Models for Strategic Thinking* (2011), offer design protocols (each with a visual illustration) as models for working through the chaos of messy decisionmaking and allowing participants to concentrate on what is most important. The gift of their little book is that the diagrams provide a quick reference, making it a flexible tool for groups. These authors summarized, "Models do not define how or what we should think; they are the result of an active thought process" (p. 6).

BENEFITS OF COLLECTIVE EFFICACY

Through the years of working to increase participation and responsibility for successful meetings and professional learning events, the authors have learned that when meetings work well they create a sense of well-being and collective efficacy. As suggested earlier, positive relationships activate oxytocin in the brain. Such success creates what organizational development experts call a "virtuous cycle." This term refers to a cycle of positive feedback reinforcing the sense of efficacy in a group: The better a community works together, the more it wants to work together.

In Chapter 2, collective efficacy is described as an essential element in liberating leadership capacity. This factor activates the will to evolve as a leadership community. When groups experience collective efficacy, they believe in their capacity to produce results and are willing to persist, even when the work is challenging. Groups experience an alignment of energies, focus, and purpose, and thus are dogged in pursuing shared outcomes. Learning and adapting through experiences reinforce the group's ability to produce collective results.

Goddard, Hoy, and Woolfolk Hoy (2004) emphasized the value of teachers' collective efficacy on the culture of the school. They found that when teachers engage in instructionally relevant school decisions, these collective actions foster a sense of organizational efficacy. As collective efficacy expands, group members respond in a variety of thinking styles. It is important to pay attention to the quality of collective thinking by asking shared questions: As a group, are we able to probe deeply? Are we speaking our truths? Are we becoming more knowledgeable about our profession? Are we becoming wise? Such thinking pervades a vibrant leadership community.

CONCLUSION

Leadership capacity is liberated within a group or organization when participants understand the value and power of generative conversations and practice them together. One conversation can change the direction of a community. These processes contribute to the creation of coherent, practice-based knowledge and to a culture of inquiry. In the next chapter, the processes of collaboration lead to one of its major purposes—the generation of knowledge.

QUESTIONS FOR PERSONAL REFLECTION

1. Review Figure 4.1 and informally assess your understandings of each of these core areas. Select one skill area and describe two learning goals.
2. Consider next steps to enhance collaborative work. Research protocols and choose one. Ask yourself: What criteria did I use for selection?
3. Review the sections of this chapter on working agreements and create an agenda for developing group agreements.
4. Using Figure 4.2, diagnose your group's performances in the dimensions of collaboration. How might you find allies who would join you in suggesting some ways to restructure your work? What would be your first steps?

Questions for Group Reflection

1. Using Figure 4.2, ask participants to silently identify an area of group strength. Ask them to identify two to three specific examples from recent meetings that support their claim and report out. Collect these data on a large chart, sorting by the four dimensions.
2. During one of your team meetings, tally the number of pauses, paraphrases, and questions. Share with your team and discuss.
3. Collect data on conversational flows—discussion, dialogue, and deliberation—and reflect on how different types of conversations shape the participatory process.

CHAPTER 5

Democratization of Knowledge

The concept of leadership capacity turns traditional leadership hierarchies on their sides, placing all participants at the center of leadership communities. The purposes of these communities reside in the definition of constructivist leadership: fostering capacity through the complex, dynamic processes of purposeful, reciprocal learning. Democratic processes create opportunities for all stakeholders to be leaders—all are capable of generating professional learning and knowledge. While the previous chapter focused on the relationships and communication patterns of community, this chapter centers on the generative qualities of learning that produces collective knowledge. The challenge is: How do communities and organizations increase their leadership capacities by generating and sustaining knowledge?

Traditionally, schools and teachers were vested as knowledge dispensers, with students as receivers of knowledge. The popular notion of the purpose of schooling during most of the 20th century was to insert knowledge—often referred to as "the canon"—into the minds of students. Knowledge was viewed as static and easily transmittable. As fields of knowledge grew and the desire to honor all voices as possessing a rightful place in a democracy took precedence, the social agreements about what constituted a common knowledge base, and what should be taught, came under scrutiny. Within this context, the debates grew as groups held onto their silos of knowledge and bumped up against one another in what became known as the "curriculum wars."

Meanwhile, the explosion of resources on the Internet and the information economy challenged the notion that knowledge was a "base" or a "what" to be determined and debated. Instead, what emerged was a vast storehouse of information in which the context, or the "field," changed the relationship of educators and citizens to knowledge. The question changed from "What is knowledge?" to "Where is knowledge?" (Thomas & Brown, 2011). Instead of asking, "How do we perfect knowledge?" the question became, "How do we organize it?" Before venturing into this bold new frontier of knowledge generation, it is helpful to consider the struggles that went before.

WHAT IS KNOWLEDGE?

Knowledge is difficult to define since its etymology emerges out of a 3,000-year-old inquiry into the depth of human experiences—how meaning and understanding are constructed, acquired, and sustained. Consequently, this robust history complicates attempts to provide a concise definition. The etymology of knowledge can be traced to a 12th-century Old English verb meaning *to acknowledge*. It was not until the 14th century that knowledge came to be used as a noun to describe an *organized body of information*, a key definition still in use today. Latin introduces into English a host of derivatives, which describe ways of knowing or branches of knowledge. Consider the similarity of these Latin words to the English derivatives: *cognito, conscientia, disciplina, doctrina, eruditio, historia, intellectus, perspicientia,* and *scientia*. From the Greek comes another derivative, *episteme*. Indeed, in 1856 a Scottish philosopher, James Ferrier, coined the English word *epistemology* to explicate the parameters of specific bodies of knowledge. Fastforward to the present, and Carla Hesse, a Stanford University historian, has defined knowledge for the 21st century as follows: "Knowledge is no longer that which is contained in space, but that which passes through it, like a series of vectors, each having direction and duration yet without precise location or limit" (quoted in Thomas & Brown, 2012, slide 4).

Drawing from this complex history, it is useful from a constructivist perspective to consider knowledge as information to which meaning is attributed. This definition recognizes that information does not become knowledge until it is meaningful to the learner—this is the process of "knowing." A conceptual itinerary in the journey toward a deeper understanding of knowing can be found in the interpretations of Kegan and Lahey's (2009) four "ways of knowing." These archetypes can be related to the ones characterizing low to high leadership capacity schools presented in Chapter 2. Kegan (1982, 1994)—and constructivist theory—suggests that in humans and in organizations, cognitive schemas and language frames at each stage of development shape the capacity to know. Accordingly, the way knowledge is valued and acted upon shapes and is shaped by the cultures described in each of the four archetypes, as follows:

1. **Low Leadership Capacity:** Appointed leaders are autocratic; knowledge is constructed and delivered by unquestioned authority. In this culture, an institutional mindset reinforces a dependency on someone else who knows best. (Kegan's instrumental mindset)
2. **Fragmented Leadership Capacity:** Knowledge is situated in the social fabric; hence privileged access to knowledge is based on power, authority, and loyalties. In these cultures, those in power work to reinforce and sustain fragmented social agreements, which

seal off subcommunities and limit learning opportunities. (Kegan's socialized mindset)

3. **Limited Leadership Capacity:** As many adults develop, they begin to question the "one right answer" or the limitation of "self-reinforcing" communities and want more than the status quo. At this point they begin to self-author a future, opening up knowledge to new possibilities. This ability to self-author requires systematic reflection on panoramic viewpoints, wherein the learner is motivated to join with others in pursuit of skills and participation opportunities. While as leaders these learners attempt to reach out to those outside the group and expand the knowledge circle, the tendency is to seek like-minded colleagues, which limits learning to self-selected groups. (Kegan's self-authoring mindset)

4. **High Leadership Capacity:** This final stage, self-transforming, changes the very nature of the capacity to know. As communities learn to deal with complex and uncertain demands of both learning and leading, they reflect more deeply about the multiplicities of knowing. There are no longer single ideologies but fields of ideologies that can be linked and understood in the context of one another. Transforming cultures are highly networked within the context of wholeness or systems within systems, those that are part of a nested system. In high capacity schools, polarized viewpoints are seen as opportunities to explore the deep, underlying assumptions that constitute knowledge, linking disparate ideas together. The ability to generate new understandings and create meaning from disparate viewpoints brings forth consilience, which is the hallmark of a transforming system. (Kegan's self-transforming mindset)

In order to build capacity, learning emerges into communal knowledge; and, as noted above, how a community approaches this task arises from the social contract. Furthermore, these conflicting developmental viewpoints about knowledge are not unique to schools, but also are played out on national and global levels. To illustrate, we draw from the recent call by the American Educational Research Association (AERA) for action to organize and sustain knowledge fields.

AN INTERNATIONAL CALL FOR TRANSFORMATION

For the centennial of the founding of the organization in 1916, the AERA in 2015 proposed that the association collectively generate a public knowledge base. The "Call for Knowledge and Findings" (AERA, 2015) is an example of how an organization might coordinate efforts to evoke leadership in a generative future. The AERA states, "The objective of this call is to cast the widest possible net across cohorts of scholars to identify significant nuggets of knowledge that span contexts, levels, and processes of education and learning" (2015, para. 3). This call may limit itself by the notion of "nuggets" and is in need of fields of knowledge that bring forth a collective voice, together inviting a fluid leadership community. Such communities could broker these knowledge fields, with the potential to change the way knowledge is constituted.

Of critical importance in this call to action is the emphasis on collective ownership and public scholarship. As outlined, AERA plans to use "crowd sourcing," a social media platform, to collect feedback and enhance an already democratic process with additional public input. This call brings forth the complex, dynamic systems of research from the community and proposes that, through reciprocal public processes, capacity can be fostered by the generation of a shared knowledge base. The AERA suggested that a possible outcome would be "to create a reservoir of important discoveries, concepts, method, and measures that evolved in recent years from education research, can enlarge public understandings, and are ripe for application in policy or practice" (2015, para. 1). This collective knowledge generation has the potential to bridge the divide between research and practice and, more important, begin the process of creating an integrated repository of knowledge, brokered by both practitioners and researchers. With the advent of the information explosion, with knowledge now fluid, and with overlapping fields, many people are studying similar concepts and using different terminology. Hence, knowing how to acquire, generate, and sustain knowledge becomes the central work of leadership communities.

Reconceptualizing knowledge flattens the hierarchy of knowledge production and engages all with interest in the quest and time. Traditionally, practitioners have not been recognized as having "knowledge" to offer researchers. Most important, this divide between research-based and practice-based knowledge continues to be problematic. Conventional attempts to bring research-based knowledge into classrooms have not yielded a systematic way to help teachers translate research into practice (Grimmett & MacKinnon, 1992; Hiebert, Gallimore, & Stigler, 2002; Huberman, 1989; Richardson & Placier, 2001).

INTEGRATING RESEARCH AND PRACTICE

As described earlier, traditional professional development often was focused not on sustained knowledge construction and acquisition, but rather on the newest trends or mandated reform efforts. Fortunately, Every Student Succeeds reaffirms the notion of sustained professional learning. In 2002, Hiebert et al. posed a question about the lack of an agreed-upon knowledge base in the title of their article: "What Would It Look Like and How Can We Get One?" They point out that the teaching profession, in the United States particularly, is limited in regard to a unified knowledge base such as may be found in other professions. Law and medicine, for instance, often organize knowledge around case studies. Attempts have been made to bring case studies into education (Barnes, Christensen, & Hansen, 1994; Lieberman, 1995). While the professional learning community movement has fostered collaboration, the Annenberg Institute for School Reform (2004) observed that these communities are often fragmented due to shifting demands, rarely sustaining long-term inquiry into practice. Without a reliable framework with which to anchor collective learning, teacher knowledge bases are often local and lacking in cohesion, therefore becoming idiosyncratic maps. An infrastructure for capturing and creating knowledge is essential so knowledge can be shared and accumulated in meaningful patterns, thereby allowing teachers to immediately practice what they are coming to understand.

Researchers, policymakers, and practitioners continue to grapple with how to bring the generative power of practitioners into the process of developing a knowledge base that can be used to ground educational practices. Cochran-Smith and Lytle (1999) provide a useful hierarchy for defining these different dimensions of knowing. Rather than using developmental models as a basis, these authors focus on the locus of the knowledge—research or practice—and suggest a hybrid blend of the two. They distinguish among knowledge *for/in/of* practices as follows:

- Knowledge-*for*-practice consists of conventional research studies and related theories, which meet strict criteria for research design and are distributed through universities, professional journals, dissertations, and conferences.
- Knowledge-*in*-practice often is called "craft knowledge" and has been criticized because of its limited, local scope. Craft knowledge emerges from practice and lives with a single teacher, group, school, or district.
- Knowledge-*of*-practice democratizes knowledge by declaring the teacher as the agent of and interpreter leading to knowledge creation. Key questions always open to discussion are: (1) What does generating knowledge mean? (2) Who generates it? (3) What counts as knowledge? and (4) How is knowledge used and evaluated?

Knowledge-for-Practice

Knowledge-for-practice is the formal knowledge and theory developed by researchers. Hiebert et al. (2002) emphasize that teachers routinely do not look for formal research or translate it into practice. However, examples can be found in the literature in which carefully designed support has demonstrated that, with guidance, teachers can interpret and utilize research to improve practices (Berliner, 1986; Carpenter, Fennema, Franke, Levi, & Empson, 2000). Despite attempts to bridge this "research into classroom gap," there appears to be little lasting impact.

In 2001, No Child Left Behind mandated reforms based on research-based practices. Initially, when the guidelines for the What Works Clearinghouse (WWC) (ies.ed.gov/ncee/wwc/) were outlined by the federal Institute of Education Sciences, many applauded. The clearinghouse was to be a repository for research-based studies that would guide educators toward best practices. Now, more than 14 years later, the clearinghouse's list of research findings about interventions is limited to a relatively small set of programs such as Reading Recovery or Open Court Reading, which must be used in their entirety in order to acquire the results promised.

Notably, well-respected researchers such as Schoenfield (2006) and Slavin (2007) were scathing in their criticism of the narrow research designs utilized by the clearinghouse. Slavin critiqued the clearinghouse for "arcane and poorly justified procedures that produced information neither scientifically justified nor useful to educators" (p. 27). Many educators, like reading researcher (and contributor to the WWC) Timothy Shanahan (2015), recommend the clearinghouse to educators with reservations. Shanahan noted that there is no easy way to determine whether the program in question was implemented effectively; hence he recommends the WWC as a guide. However, the Investing in Innovation Fund uses the WWC standards as criteria for the grants awarded, despite their narrow focus (Deborah Walker, personal communication, July 10, 2015). Despite the criticism and the resources allocated to the effort, WWC has not significantly evolved and therefore has contributed little to an educational knowledge base.

The Common Core State Standards, adopted and renamed by many states, are another example of an attempt to move research theory into practice. The writers of the CCSS cited scholarly research, as well as surveys, assessment data, and international comparisons, in the development of the standards. Since these standards emerged out of a synthesis, the research rationale is not always evident. Chapter 4 described the concept of ongoing inquiry into the meaning of the CCSS and how it shaped practices at Oak Valley Middle School. Later in this chapter, another school system is described that utilized the research into the standards to build communal knowledge.

Knowledge-in-Practice

Knowledge-in-practice is the knowledge gleaned from the classroom through years of practice and interaction with students. Over the past 15 years, with all of the external mandates accompanying standards and assessment implementation, little attention has been paid to the knowledge acquired by teachers during years in the classroom. Costa, Garmston, and Zimmerman (2014) describe the knowledge in teachers' heads as valuable *cognitive capital*, the rich thinking occurring in the minds of teachers. Teachers' practice-based competencies far exceed the scope of the CCSS and include, to name just a few, knowledge of content, classroom management, child development, learning trajectories, differentiation, and student engagement. In each setting as well, teacher knowledge involves how to work with colleagues and parents.

In leadership communities, however, teachers are primarily in charge of their inquiries into practice and this inquiry is communal, thereby building capacities within the community. Notably, there is a growing number of regional knowledge-in-practice consortia, such as the National Writing Project (www.nwp.org) and Education Northwest (educationnorthwest.org/traits/trait-definitions), that disseminate practice-based knowledge. In Australia, such ventures include the Project for Enhancing Effective Learning (PEEL) and the Perspective and Voice of the Teacher (PAVOT). Even though the Australian PEEL program was unfunded and was not the result of an institutional-level initiative, it gained momentum. Thirty years after implementation, the process continues to prove rewarding enough to operate as a network of autonomous groups of teachers. Focusing on a shared purpose for active learning and innovative classroom-tested teaching procedures, PEEL attained coherence in knowledge construction rarely found in other systems. Teachers share their knowledge in a journal entitled *PEEL Seeds*, workshops, books about the project, and PEEL in Practice, a large database gleaned over 30 years (www.peelweb.org).

Wenger (1998) has developed another promising line of inquiry into practice through *communities of practice*. These communities, as described in Chapter 3, are emergent and self-organizing, arising from jointly defined explorations into practice. When communities combine their practices, resources, and perspectives, they develop a shared sense of purpose and identity. They reveal an ongoing need to know what others know. Communities of practice create, refine, communicate, and use knowledge. These communities can serve to transfer the knowledge to larger communities. For example, several large agencies such as the National Writing Project and Education Northwest have served as brokers for practice-based knowledge about writing as a process.

When learning communities and other professional learning designs focus on practice-based knowledge, they adopt new, more fluid ideas of how knowledge is constructed. Teachers report great satisfaction in learning designs focused on collaborative inquiries into practice. Before the advent of the Internet, teachers had limited abilities to collect and share this knowledge. Now with the use of social networking programs, knowledge can be shared within the larger profession.

Knowledge-of-Practice

Cochran-Smith and Lytle (1999) offer a third path—knowledge-of-practice— which does not separate formal from practical knowledge, but views collective inquiry as the vital link. This knowledge is constructed in learning communities engaged in intentional investigation, inquiring into both their own and others' practices, as well as published research and theory.

Knowledge-of-practice is generative in that the reciprocal processes guiding the task of collectively coming to know emerges from inquiry within a learning community. Bringing collective agency into the learning process liberates leadership capacities and unites educators as equals. As noted earlier, when inquiry becomes embedded in a high leadership capacity culture, it is systemic, collaborative, and sustaining. This democratic perspective of the knowledge–practice continuum places teachers in charge of their professional lives.

GENERATING KNOWLEDGE

Through the drive to generate knowledge, teachers adopt a critical perspective of practice, theory, and research; they co-join with peers, and often researchers as well, to discover practice-based exemplars; they open avenues for conversations that extend knowledge. Professional learning informs and is informed by teachers' knowledge of and inquiry into practice, and becomes an important investment in the development of communal learning. The process of generating knowledge in high leadership capacity communities through inquiry is deeply connected to sustainability. Indeed it is in these conversations that teachers learn about one another's deep thinking and beliefs about practice, and grow their investment in both leadership and learning. Hargreaves and Fullan (2012) extend the concept of investing to the development of professional capital. Human capital development requires investment in leadership actions, career stages, and collective contributions; social capital suggests that when the group changes group behaviors, this represents the most powerful form of investment. Costa et al. (2014) expand the metaphor of professional capital to include "cognitive capital"—the development of the cognitive capacity of the individual and the organization. This developmental process unfolds and flourishes in community, fostering the ability to work with more complex ideas and to draw forth new knowledge informing practice.

Capitalizing on Specialized Knowledge in Community

When Aretha, the principal of Oak Valley Middle School, first assumed her new position, the low performance scores on the 7th-grade, state-mandated writing assessment surprised her. As a result, she invited English teachers to join her in a collaborative inquiry to discover why the scores were so low. Joan, one of the English teachers, clearly stood apart as a resident expert. While most other teachers were using variations of the state-adopted litera-ture series, Joan excitedly described how her favorite teacher-researchers and writers had become her long-distance mentors—individuals from across the country who had created a literacy knowledge base and published their work.

As Joan spoke, she held up dog-eared copies of books written by teacher-writers Nancie Atwell (1998), Ralph Fletcher (2011), Carol Jago (2002), and Laura Robb (2010). She explained that a friend from another school had invited her to a book study of Nancie Atwell's *In the Middle: New Under-standings About Writing, Reading, and Learning* 4 years ago. This 6-week collaboration had shifted Joan's writing instruction from the practice of stu-dents writing alone to working with peers. Not only had this change im-proved student writing; it had opened creative choices for her teaching. For example, when students became excited about the humor in a peer's writing, these class members began to add humor to their own writings as well. Other teachers at Oak Valley were intrigued and suggested they collaborate in a book study group. The English teachers at Oak Valley asked Joan to pick her favorite resource to begin their inquiry into writing practices.

While driving home, Aretha reflected on the inequities created when teachers work in isolation. It was clear that students in Joan's English classes had qualitatively different learning experiences. This concern strengthened her resolve to work with teachers in order to create the conditions whereby they could lead their own learning. Further, while Joan clearly had expertise, Aretha knew that, once teachers began conversing on topics that mattered, they soon would be learning from one another. When teachers have an op-portunity to design their own learning experiences, it changes their relation-ships to one another, to learning, to leadership—and to knowledge.

Generating Knowledge Fields

Joan had not realized it, but when she decided to study the writings of Nancie Atwell (whose story appears in Chapter 3), she joined a community of learners that over time developed their own field of knowledge about literacy. Her learning path highlighted an unusual twist in curricular history instructive for the broader understanding of knowledge construction. In the 1980s, a new paradigm of teacher-as-researcher began with Don Graves and the National Institute of Education. Graves joined 1st-grade teacher Mary Ellen Glacobbe in studying the development of emergent writers. This research, situating the teacher as a producer-of-knowledge, found a willing home in a small offshoot of a British publishing company, Heinemann, and later Stenhouse. Most notable in this story is the democratization of knowledge by teacher-researchers-turned-writers; the publishers were pivotal in sustaining the resulting knowledge base.

Moreover, the emphasis on the student–teacher exchange pioneered by Graves was essential to the sustained interest of teachers in this work. These teacher-writers focused on real problems of practice and described not only what they did, but also how the students responded. These books were infused with rich, accessible descriptions of student actions. Armed with robust classroom descriptions from Lucy Calkins (1994), Nancie Atwell (1998), Katie Wood Ray (1999), and many more, teachers found influential mentors—an important resource for learning. Through reading, reflection, and action, these teachers developed their own unique knowledge fields that not only enlightened, but also deepened their cognitive capacity to engage in the creation of deep collective understandings.

A knowledge *base* is distinct from a knowledge *field*. A traditional definition of knowledge focused on a fixed "knowledge base"—something to acquire more often than not from experts. To advance a conceptualization of knowledge as generative, knowledge fields are considered reciprocal and composed of a multiplicity of fields in which each person and discipline holds a unique perspective. Knowledge forms a feedback loop, being reflected back, examined, and expanded in community to create robust knowledge. Through the reciprocal interactions in high leadership capacity schools, these fields become more visible and enfold into a shared sense of purpose and vision informed by practice.

Generating Knowledge for Leadership Capacity

When the editors of *The Reading Teacher* asked educational researchers Johnston and Goatley (2014/2015) to identify the literacy research most impacting classroom practices, they cited the genre of books described above, which focuses on rich descriptions of literacy practices. While traditional researchers often dismissed teacher-generated knowledge, Johnston and Goatley, in contrast, raised the question: What is research if it does not impact and improve daily practice in the classroom?

Taking responsibility for developing communal knowledge changes the nature of knowledge exploration into an active process of thinking through questions of practice. For the educators described above, knowledge for teaching was no longer fixed, but rather a complex, dynamic process in which reciprocal interactions informed practices. While many curriculum leaders were aware of this parallel literacy movement, and brought teacher-recommended videos into professional learning, the depth of these teachers' knowledge was not often mined in a way that contributed to the larger community.

Joan developed a robust and generative knowledge field, which she drew from regularly to think about teaching. She thought of teaching as a reciprocal act and asked often, "Am I getting the responses I want from my students? And if not, how will I adapt?" Likewise, design thinking provides leadership communities with reflection tools focused on the capacities of observation, experimentation, iteration, and risk-taking with which to test and adapt new ideas in the classroom. For teachers like Joan, this continuous redesign process is embedded into her teaching and is ongoing, occurring in every teaching event.

These insights and the deepened practices of Joan and others like her demonstrate the power of ongoing, focused collaboration for building coherent knowledge fields. In his work on the development of the social network knowledge platform known as Declara, González (2014b) and his team discovered success when "innovation" communities worked on "concrete fractal problems of practice small enough to be manageable operationally, but large enough to encompass the systemic nature of the desired change" (p. 7). González elegantly echoed what Joan and her colleagues understood: When focused on specific learning elements, the response created a fractal that informed the similar yet different adaptations. This learning-centered practice gives rise to classroom innovations that are then shared with colleagues. González calls for practitioner-centered co-designs, augmented by technologies, to create agile collaboration and credible evidence, which in turn create other designs for learning.

In low leadership capacity schools, expertise remains hidden, with teachers continuing to work in isolation without the benefit of building collaborative knowledge. Design thinking and social network platforms like Declara have the potential to call forth teacher knowledge and recognize expertise as one important resource for communal knowledge development. In contrast, low leadership capacity schools, which are often devoid of professional conversations, frequently fail to recognize the expertise of peers; hence the capacity to learn remains static. Systems theory provides an apt metaphor: In low leadership capacity schools, knowledge is not viewed as a resource and hence is not harvested and shared, but rather is squandered and lost, creating what is called the "tragedy of the commons."

Constructing Knowledge Through Networked Communities

In Washoe County, Nevada, the mandate was clear: implement the Common Core State Standards. Under the leadership of Aaron Grossman, a teacher appointed on special assignment to lead this charge, the teachers learned how to become inquiring leaders (Morones, 2014). Coming from a teaching perspective, Grossman was not interested in giving answers, but rather in finding forums for inviting teachers to find their own answers. Early in this process he struggled; he found discussions about the standards were unnecessarily challenging. Grossman felt strongly that the questions arising in the debates over the CCSS needed to be answered by the teachers who were posing the questions; they needed to inquire for themselves. To jump-start the process, he went directly to the source via the Internet and provided unfiltered information so teachers could review the rationale for the standards and arrive at their own interpretations. This process led the teachers to take responsibility for experimenting with what they were learning about the CCSS. As they reflected and dialogued together, the standards took on new meanings. These small studies grew into "Core Practices" posted on the Internet. When answers could not be found, the group reached out and created a network link with the coauthors of the literacy standards, David and Meredith Liben. Soon the group was collaborating with the Libens to create short videos, which were shared through iTunes, further extending the network. Not only would teachers inside the system continue to collaborate, but these resources also were available via the Internet for other teachers as well. This story is a complement to the Oak Valley inquiry into the standards.

Grossman's (personal communication, May 17, 2014) approach tells how a teacher on special assignment, given a clear mandate, designed inquiries that emboldened teachers to create their own knowledge in collaboration with one another and the authors of the CCSS. This initiative expanded through teacher networking, and soon the collaborators grew to more than 1,000 teachers. While Grossman, as a teacher on special assignment, took the lead for designing the initial inquiry, it was the classroom teachers who advocated for more of this inquiry-based learning design and spread the word across the county. Grossman also developed an online repository for their work in the Core Task Project (63000resources.com/core-task-project/), in which teachers were able to publish CCSS lessons. While the entire school district was not involved in this change effort, this story reveals how high capacity learning can exist as a subset of a larger community. As Grossman prepares to return to the classroom, and while excited to be back with students, he also knows his future lies in more opportunities to work with leadership communities.

Through the exploration of knowledge fields, teachers make classrooms and schools sites for collective inquiry and create mental maps or schemas that attribute meaning to their discoveries. They are self-authoring their teaching future, both as individuals and in a networked community. Furthermore, these inquiry approaches benefit from linking to the wider world of knowledge about teaching and learning. It is important that educators extend their inquiry beyond the boundaries of the school. Networked inquiry can be initiated by all—and initiation is a primary hallmark of leadership.

Heinz von Forester, lauded as a pioneer of systems theory, gave credit for his expansive knowledge to others. Forever humble, he acknowledged the collaborative community he joined in Chicago after fleeing Austria during World War II. As he explained, when you rub shoulders with other smart people, you learn what they know. In his view, collaboratively learned knowledge was the essence of intelligence (personal communication, August 26, 1997). It is also the essence of reciprocity.

High leadership capacity communities demonstrate the power of collective innovation as well as the personal learning agility of each participant. Those at policy levels would do well to create policies and practices that develop and sustain teacher networks, inquiry communities, and other school-based collectives in which practitioners co-join in their efforts to construct knowledge.

SUSTAINING KNOWLEDGE

Until recently it has been difficult for communities of teachers to capture, retain, and share knowledge in meaningful ways. In the decades before the Internet, when teachers generated knowledge, the avenues for sharing were severely limited. Aaron Grossman commented that finding a way to organize information and make it accessible has proved challenging. He used a blog as a way of summarizing the group's accomplishments, but found its use limited, since blogs usually are organized by date, not topic.

With the advent of the Internet and social networking, there are more and more ways for individuals and groups to form communities organized around a few central ideas. Social media create the opportunity for connectivity with others, information discovery and sharing, and personal collection and adaptation of information (McLoughlin & Lee, 2010). New social networking sites emerge continually, rendering the generation, collection, and curating of information easier.

While learning communities usually occur in real time, the possibilities posited by Web 2.0 and the wide application of video via YouTube are just beginning to be fully realized. The Internet will continue to change the face of knowledge in ways not yet understood or imagined. In the grand scheme of information, the Internet provides a new conception of knowledge acquisition and construction. When educators leverage rich web resources to develop knowledge bases that serve local and global networks, the potential for professional capacity is unparalleled.

Democratizing Knowledge—Wikipedia

Once thought of as an online encyclopedia, Wikipedia has proven to be more of a gateway to knowledge than a definitive source. While debates continue about the reliability of the sources, the fact remains that by 2005 Wikipedia had become the most popular reference website on the Internet. Revolutionary at the time, the founders organized the website using "wiki," a simple format for developing web content, allowing virtually anyone with knowledge and time to engage in communal knowledge construction and generation. What often is misunderstood about Wikipedia in its ever-changing state is that its backstory includes detailed records of controversies—including discussions, resolutions, and alterations. This resource, with almost 40 million editors, has behind-the-scenes collaboration tools, such as talk pages, available history of edits, and a system for dispute resolution among editors.

The multi-contributor format of Wikipedia has continued to defy conventional definitions of knowledge generation. With its networked contribution structure, Wikipedia has democratized knowledge. When used as gateway source for knowledge, it provides overviews, descriptions of practice, and citations designed to take a reader to original sources. When scholars and practitioners alike contribute to Wikipedia, they add well-researched citations and can weigh in on controversies in a detailed "talk page."

In a 2009 MacArthur Foundation Report, Davidson and Goldberg claim that a pillar for learning in the 21st century is to learn not to trust a presumed authority, but to learn how to assess the collective credibility of a source. They argue: "To ban sources such as Wikipedia is to miss the importance of collaborative, knowledge-making impulse in humans who are willing to contribute, correct and collect information without remuneration: by definition, this *is* education" (p. 29, emphasis in original). While Wikipedia has stood a short test of time, it remains to be seen how it will further influence the global generation of knowledge.

Knowledge Fields

Knowledge is an emergent phenomenon in which what we come to know in community coalesces into fields upon fields of deeper knowledge. Carla Hesse suggested: "In the future, it seems, there will be no fixed canons of texts and no fixed epistemological boundaries between disciplines, only paths of inquiry, modes integration, and moments of encounter" (quoted in Thomas & Brown, 2012, slide 4).

Although the authors had written together before, as we created this book, we did not fully appreciate the divergent knowledge fields each of us brought to the project. As these differences bumped up against one another, disagreements arose and had to be worked through. Out of this process grew new understandings fitting together in coherent ways to build even more fields of knowledge. The spaces between these fields allowed for an exploration of learning edges. It was as if the spaces between knowledge fields created new possibilities not previously considered. Consequently, the content of this book is a result of reciprocal interactions among various forms of knowledge.

These various forms of knowledge from which the authors drew inspiration for decades are the essential value of an interdisciplinary worldview. The social sciences, physical sciences, humanities, and performing arts all interconnect to create knowledge fields. Without this synthesis of knowledge, leadership could not be understood within the context of complex, dynamic systems.

Multiplicities of knowing—fields of linked knowledge—are creatively understood in the context of one another. This highly networked way of understanding honors the first Old English definition of knowledge—to acknowledge. Honoring, acknowledging, and appreciating the tremendous capacity of the human spirit to continuously push the boundaries of knowledge fields release learners into a never-ending search for meaning. The 13th-century mystic poet Rumi said it well:

> Out beyond ideas of wrongdoing and right doing,
> There is a field. I'll meet you there.
> When the soul lies down in that grass,
> The world is too full to talk about.
> Ideas, language, and even the phrase "each other"
> doesn't make any sense.

BEYOND EXPLICIT KNOWLEDGE

Generative knowledge grows in community. By situating constructivist learning and leading in these reciprocal processes, a primary leadership goal becomes the generation of communal knowledge fields. Knowledge is a topic for reflective conversations through which it emerges into fields of knowledge informing high capacity expertise.

Much of learning comes from doing, watching, and experiencing—often called tacit knowing. While learners may be conscious of what they are learning in community, they may not fully appreciate that, through the capacity to absorb meaningful information from the environment, humans develop significant knowledge. In the Reggio Children example in Chapter 3, "experience" is considered the third teacher in the room. It is always the third teacher. Consider the testimony of Patrice Bryan and stories of teacher learning drawn from other cultures: Honduras, Guatemala, and Picasso's hometown, Málaga, Spain. Experience in dissimilar cultures creates dissonance, which questions our knowing, and shifts our understandings.

Tacit knowledge, learned outside of language, may not become easily explicit. Yet, in a high leadership capacity school, tacit knowledge is made explicit. To illustrate the dynamic capacities of tacit knowledge, Zimmerman recalled the moment when, as a facilitator, she shifted from time-driven agendas to outcome-driven agendas. It was not until she was asked, "What do you mean by an outcome-driven agenda?" that she realized how nuanced her learning had become. She stumbled over her own words, "Groups have a way of shifting energy that suggests they are ready to transition." When probed for more, Zimmerman rethought what she had said. "Well, that is not really it. I learned to give directions that anticipated the transitions, and then I watched for movement towards those transitions. . . . It is hard to put this into words, but when you know the outcomes, you observe with those outcomes in mind and make transitions based on group responses rather than time." This story reveals fine distinctions in tacit knowledge. Zimmerman had not learned this knowledge from a book, but from working with others who knew how to make these distinctions. She learned by watching and doing. As individuals gain in expertise, their actions communicate through modeling, a primary means by which teachers and principals learn to lead in learning communities.

CONCLUSION

In this chapter, the conceptual journey situated knowledge as an emergent concept. Indeed, the way knowledge is constructed, valued, and acted upon shapes and is shaped by community (Kegan & Lahey, 2009). At each stage in the development of leadership capacity, cognitive schemas and the resultant language define knowledge. In low capacity schools, experts deliver knowledge as if it were a package, and hence the overt language is of acceptance and acquiescence. In contrast, in high leadership capacity schools with flatter hierarchies, communities engage in systematic reflection in which knowledge is constructed, organized, and networked. In the stories of Oak Valley Middle School and Washoe County, Nevada, learning communities drew strength from their growing sense of efficacy, emergent awareness, flexibility, and interdependence.

In Chapter 6, discussions of systemic change and questions of sustainability are accompanied by stories of high leadership capacity schools and systems within the United States and globally. These examples merge understandings of the underlying factors giving rise to alternative paths to improvement and the roads undertaken toward whole-system transformation. Transformation arises organically and unpredictably rather than being imposed from above, for change is a natural process. The reciprocal cycles of learning unleash these natural processes and emerge into high leadership capacity schools and organizations.

QUESTIONS FOR PERSONAL REFLECTION

1. Review the four archetypes of leadership capacity presented in Figure 2.1 in Chapter 2 and compare these to the four "ways of knowing" as defined by Kegan above. Select one of the archetypes and the accompanying way of knowing. What does this tell you about knowledge development in your own school or organization?
2. Create a chart with three columns: knowledge for, knowledge in, and knowledge of. Reflect on one of the most pivotal learning experiences in your career. Identify which type of knowledge was developed and list the experience in the appropriate column. How does this process inform your future work in leadership communities?
3. Reflect on the experiences at Oak Valley School in which Joan took the initial leadership role. Are there individuals in your school whom you might turn to as learning partners? How would you initiate the conversation?

QUESTIONS AND ACTIVITY FOR GROUP REFLECTION

1. As a group, consider question 2, above. Discuss these three types of knowledge and identify two to three next steps for broadening the construction of knowledge in your school or organization.
2. Conduct a Social Network Fair in which teachers share the different ways they use the Internet to network with others. Agree to try out one platform for a month and evaluate.

CHAPTER 6

Creating Capacity for Systems Change

Change is a natural outcome of reciprocal human interactions in complex systems. Such interactions weave patterns of relationships calling forth intention, collective agency, and innovation. We have seen how the web-like image of a high leadership capacity school or organization forms a buoyant, resilient culture from which any individual or set of individuals could leave, and the web reconnects behind them, forming a wholeness once again.

As noted earlier, a prime barrier to the development of complex systems lies in isolation and separation, both factors a result of the lack of diversity—of people, ideas, places, spaces. Classrooms, schools, departments, and other "silos," as well as isolation wrought by vast geographical terrains, inhibit essential interactions. Isolation from diversity—homogeneous schools, organizations, and communities—is among the most problematic of conditions. Therefore, such systems must be artfully re-created through connection, communication, and collaborative learning designs.

In 1995, the authors of *The Constructivist Leader* (Lambert et al.) invoked the metaphor of "sea change" for the processes advocated therein. It is still an apt metaphor. Feedback spirals, propelled by reciprocal learning in community, is the sea moving in upon itself. Shifts forward occur through the dynamic of meaning-making. This recursive process is an essential dimension of complexity: The whole folds into a process of learning and re-learning. For instance, within a school staff, dialogue may lead to inquiry, the findings of which alter the next conversation; learning becomes deeper and deeper as new perspectives are discovered. This is a self-organizing process—the central concept of systemic change.

Leadership fosters capacity through the complex, dynamic processes of purposeful, reciprocal learning. Leadership capacity situates leadership in the intersections of participation and skillfulness, giving rise to the crucial roles played by administrators, teachers, students, parents, and community members. Sustainability is the crucial outcome of high leadership capacity. These perspectives form the frameworks through which we view systemic change. The preceding chapters described how specific design processes, skills, and communities set forth the paths that propel human interactions into sustainable emergent outcomes.

SHIFTING CONCEPTIONS OF CHANGE

If change is a natural phenomenon, why is school and organizational improvement so difficult? "Change agents" sometimes have been adept at shoving round ideas into square holes. Uniform policies attempt to direct organic processes. Linear logic—setting narrow goals and objectives—and shepherding behaviors in those directions actually steers systems away from the natural processes of change. Traditional approaches consistently deal with "predetermined" aspects of goals, objectives, knowledge bases, policies, and authority distribution. Internal criteria for success place responsibility before accountability. Figure 6.1 describes traditional change processes based on linear logic, which often is referred to as "strategic planning," comparing these approaches to constructivist change processes.

Constructivist change processes arise from practice, rather than being imposed on practice. The interactions characterizing leadership communities uncover trouble spots and gaps—those performance areas falling short of achieving the school's expectations. If academic performance falls below expectations, the task is to discover why; if behaviors are less than positive, the task of an inquiring community is to unearth underlying causes. If causes are unclear, a helpful approach is to advance with bold innovations in pursuit of creative answers. A culture designed for such journeys becomes sustainable—not because of special funding or personnel, but because the members of the community learn their way to answers and become committed to what they discover. This is collective agency; these processes weave together sustainable patterns of relationships.

NESTED ADAPTIVE SYSTEMS

Education systems are nested within other systems: districts, counties, regions, states, and the nation (Figure 6.2). Echoing through these nests is the responsibility for all to interact, share information, and work together. As nested complex systems evolve with and influence one another in a nonlinear, reciprocal fashion, they provide information and feedback throughout—the sea moving in upon itself. As noted in earlier chapters, continuous professional learning and knowledge fields are major parts of such systems. Dynamic interactions give rise to an emergence of new patterns and self-organization. Fluid, yet purposeful, boundaries allow for

Figure 6.1. A Study in Contrast: The Processes of Change

Traditional Processes	Constructivist Processes
Intention is to implement specific content changes	Intention determined by shared values and meanings among peers
Predetermined knowledge base	Pluralistic knowledge bases informed by observation, inquiry, and discourse
Problem is predetermined; solutions find problems	Problem finding central to inquiring stance
Predetermined objectives based on the above processes	Objectives emerge naturally as discrepancies are understood
Innovation not mediated with current practice	Changes evolve from practice, knowledge bases, and problem finding
Prescribed skills needed by leader in content area	Skills in reciprocal processes needed by all
Participation by those who agree to or are required to adopt innovation	Multiple, sustained opportunities for participation
Training for those who adopt innovation	Participation involves professional learning
Parameters as limits, e.g., regulations, policies, contracts	Adaptive parameters serve emerging goals
Partnerships, where they exist, are hierarchical	Partnerships exist among equals
Monitored and evaluated by external criteria and agent	Self-monitoring based on internal criteria is primary
Sustainability relies on special funding and staffing	Sustainability emerges from altered patterns of relationships

Adapted from Lambert et al., 1995, Figure 3.1.

movement among cultures. Essentially nothing in the environment is fixed. In such environments, participants can anticipate the future—looking down the road at new research in brain development and learning, changes in technology, even environmentally sensitive school construction. The field of vision is opened by transparent horizons.

An example of a dynamic within the center of a nested system is the essential nature of interactions that ignite the fuel for emergence. At least three program reforms are central to combustion: one concerning relationships, one regarding a new learning approach, one related to structure. A simple formula. The Oak Valley Middle School adopted problem-based,

Figure 6.2. Nested Adaptive Systems

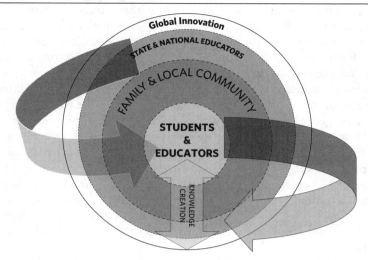

experiential learning and peer coaching, and established cross-age learning teams. The dynamic shifted relationships, cognition, and venue.

Southworth (2005) understands the dynamic of three interacting factors. He refers to "three strategies, one powerful effect" (p. 82). For Southworth, these are the leadership strategies of modeling, monitoring, and dialogue. Modeling good practice and high expectations inspires community members to excel; monitoring signals the focus of sustained attention; dialogue deepens knowledge and examines assumptions, leading to new ways of viewing the world of learning. Acting together, self-organization is propelled forward.

Assuming that schools are complex systems within larger nested systems makes adaptive policies paramount. These are policies that can "anticipate and respond to an array of conditions that lie ahead and can navigate towards successful outcomes when surprised by the unforeseen" (Venema & Drexhage, 2009, p. 2). Adaptive policies are contextual and responsive to the needs of each level of the larger system, securing the structures, procedures, and approaches needed at school, district, and organization levels (Swanson et al., 2009). Randi Weingarten (2015), American Federation of Teachers president, reported on New York's new and expanding PROSE (Progressive Redesign Opportunity Schools for Excellence) schools. These collaborative schools involve teachers as leaders and are able to adapt contract terms at the local level if the staff believes different terms will better serve their students. Thus, each layer of the nest has the freedom to assess its environments and adapt procedures and practices to meet current needs and cultures.

As noted in Figures 6.1 and 6.2, complexity dynamics are capable of spontaneously generating new structures without direction from external agents; and they often generate unpredictable outcomes because they are driven by random behaviors and complex interactions (Uhl-Bien & Marion, 2008). Both individual and collective participants can consciously generate change manifesting itself as new insights, breakthrough solutions, innovative ideas, and revised ways of understanding. Providing the conditions for a free flow of ideas and the emergence of new ideas is the role of everyone in the system, generating strong learning cultures throughout the nest.

The role of each level of the nested system is to work with all the other levels of the system to develop and use the language and processes that foster capacity, develop trust in the future, and provide space for people from diverse roles to create new paradigms. District, state, and national agencies have a scaffolding role to play in order to support the work being done at the local level. Such work involves identifying resources, garnering broad community and corporate support, and assisting as consultants with individual educators and schools.

A major responsibility of district offices and state and federal governments is to calibrate their support with what is happening at the local level. Rather than mandating how to accomplish the work of the entire educational "nested" organization, they can collect and provide access to best practice, convene educators to review and develop instructional approaches, evaluate successes, distribute ideas through websites, and arrange for cross-organizational exchanges. Flexible, adaptive policies gathered from other sites can be shared. A part of such wise calibration is to get out of the way of schools launching self-authoring, innovative work. By realizing and trusting the power of the local system, authority is dispersed.

LEADERSHIP CAPACITY AND SYSTEMIC CHANGE

The leadership capacity matrix (see Figure 2.1) reveals high leadership capacity (Figure 6.3) as a web or network of interactions emerging from the change processes described above. The descriptors of a high capacity school are drawn from research and observation of successful, sustainable schools. These descriptors, interacting together, create a loosely woven fabric capable of expansion and adaptation.

This fabric or pattern for achieving high capacity is strikingly similar to the Global Fourth Way described by Hargreaves and Shirley (2012). The Global Fourth Way is drawn from an array of successful international and national programs transcending the confining rules of traditional change (see Figure 6.1). Hargreaves and Shirley describe three interlocking elements central to coherent change. The *first* principle suggests there must

Figure 6.3. High Leadership Capacity

Archetype 4: High Capacity

- Principals and teachers, as well as parents and students, are part of generative learning communities.
- Shared vision results in program coherence and collective agency.
- Inquiry leads to growth in knowledge and improved practice.
- Roles and actions reflect collaboration, trusting relationships, networking, and collective responsibility.
- Reflective practice consistently leads to innovation.
- Student performance, based on multiple measures, is steadily improving.

be a national vision and a clear sense of where a country is going. This is a natural outgrowth of national identity. Their *second* element is a collaborative culture, involving co-leading among teachers, administrators, students, parents, and community members. Such collaboration gives rise to a vision that is heartfelt, both personally and professionally. A regard for difference and diversity among adults and students enables learners to exercise discretion, choice, and agency within the context of a collaborative culture. The *third* aspect of the Global Fourth Way is public engagement, which promotes democratic inclusion—central to the conception of leadership capacity as well. Societies and organizations create themselves through democratic discourse. In other words, professionals gain more autonomy from the government, but also less autonomy from the public, parents, and communities. Practice becomes a transparent process for conversation.

Achieving and sustaining systems change finds coherence in ideas shared by the Fourth Way and the high leadership capacity archetype. The selected international programs described below are expressions of these principles. But first, consider questions of sustainability on the national front.

Can Systems Last?

This question repeats itself like a mantra. Collins and Porras (1994) analyzed systems that were "Built to Last." Hargreaves and Fink (2006) wrote of system sustainability. Michael Fullan (2005) suggested multiple ways in which leaders might bring about sustainability. Kofi Annan, former secretary-general of the United Nations, insisted, "Education is a human right with immense power to transform. On its foundation rests the cornerstones of freedom, democracy and sustainable human development" (quoted in Humme, 2012). Yet, the barriers often seem overwhelming.

In the San Francisco Bay area, a medium-sized school district recently experienced an 88% change in administrative personnel over a 3-year period. Jan Huls, former principal of an elementary school in this district, sought to find out what had been sustained 4 years after her retirement. More than a dozen years earlier, Huls wrote about the achievements of this high leadership capacity school (Lambert et al., 2002).

In 2015, Huls discovered that the strong focus on equity, once the primary value underlying actions in the district and schools, had given way to other priorities. A visionary leadership team entitled the Dreamcatchers no longer met. However, culturally responsive teaching, viewed by teachers as deeply beneficial to students, was still in place in almost all classrooms. The new district administration was hierarchical in nature and the site leadership team met infrequently. Classroom-centered activities had more chance of survival in pockets throughout the school than in schoolwide practices requiring examination of student work, continuous conversations, and reinforcement. Other areas of shared practice, such as explicit direct instruction and professional learning communities, had unraveled.

The role of the principal and veteran teacher leaders in this Bay Area school in weaving the network together changed as the district took responsibility for choosing, training, and assigning teacher coaches and parent facilitators. The presence of the teachers union became stronger, and practices once agreed upon as "must do" shifted to "may do" throughout the district and schools. Huls concluded, "In the absence of a continuing shared vision, and with the centralization of services by the district, the school community has become more reactive rather than efficacious, a drastic shift in leadership capacity" (personal communication, June 10–15, 2015).

Ryan Land, a school board member in Manitoba, is now working in the mining industry. Land, a former principal who sought to lead his school toward leadership capacity, teacher leadership, and student achievement, was removed from his position by a close vote of the board of trustees influenced by a growing culture of fear and suppression. These individuals considered his work in sharp contrast to the conservative aims of a few entrenched community members. Forced to change professions in order to stay in the community, he was later elected to the school board by a "Landslide." When asked how he would describe the issue, he was forthright:

> Some would certainly say, perhaps rightly, that I tried to effect too much change, too soon. It's an old argument, and while there is surely some merit to it, I felt there were a number of things we could not negotiate on. The bottom line for me was that our administrative team expected a commitment to school leadership, ethical and professional behaviour, and learning from everyone, including students. A minority of fundamentalists wished to hold onto a culture of "teachers first" and the power that came along with it. Initially, perhaps the most inflammatory thing I said was that we would put "students first,"

but eventually a strong, increasingly vocal and courageous majority started to believe in it and got in behind the ideal to push. (Personal communication, May 15–22, 2015)

It is not unusual to encounter a community uncomfortable with new directions, such as the promotion of a value of equity in the Bay Area school above, a deep-rooted union, or a community that perceives itself as protecting its historical identity.

Each of these factors serves as a harbinger of reaction to change. Loucks and Hall (1979) alerted us decades ago to the counterintuitive truth that "it's good for kids" doesn't often bring commitment; concerns for self and the burden of the tasks come first. An understanding of leadership capacity leads to a concern for broad-based, skillful participation in the work of leadership: to build relationships, collaboration, reflection, trust, and mutual regard. Unearthing soil made solid and crunchy by the ages takes time. And these factors create a holding environment while evolution to higher forms of human development takes place.

When change comes smoothly and quickly, two possibilities arise: Either the change is not worth the paper it's written on, or the antecedents have created a stunning readiness, as in the stories below of Creekside and Encina schools and the Maplewood Richmond Heights district.

Succession Planning and Sustainability

One of the most critical issues in sustainability is succession planning. The concept of leadership capacity poses a few essential considerations. First, large-system personnel need to understand the arc of development of school movement(s) toward high capacity and ensure the sustained presence of key personnel until the school has moved beyond limited capacity (Archetype 3) and is firmly situated in high capacity status. Such awareness on the part of districts can prevent a successful principal or key teacher leader from being plucked out of the school too early. Second, when key personnel, such as a principal or teacher leader, leave, the larger district system involves school staff in creating the criteria for selection, and a mentoring program is inaugurated both inside and outside the school. Teachers in high leadership capacity schools are among the best mentors for new principals. Former and current principals from other successful schools make excellent mentors as well.

Two additional observations are pertinent in succession planning from a leadership capacity perspective: The system may decide to make this a self-governing school (see the story of Creekside School below) or select a principal from within the school. The latter option becomes possible in a limited or high capacity school as long as the person is a teacher leader who has helped to improve capacity.

Below, the stories of two schools and one district capture some of the more promising aspects of creating sustainable systems.

Creekside School, Black Oak Mine District, Georgetown, California. In Chapter 2, the journey of Wendy Westsmith at Northside School is described. Here, she reflects on the genesis of this work in the story of Creekside School (personal communication, June 8–21, 2015). In the beginning, Creekside was a family. As a small, rural K–5 elementary school located in the foothills of the Sierra Nevada range, Creekside was an integral part of the life of the local community, and the community was an integral part of the school decisionmaking process.

In 1995, the communal life and the departure of the onsite principal created a conversation about becoming a self-governing school, a school to be governed by teachers, parents, and stakeholders equally. While geography and small size provided an advantage in establishing intimacy within the school community, the school staff's approach to shared leadership, which Creekside called "self-governance," became the foundation of its culture. Creekside became one of a handful of public schools practicing self-governance and shared leadership led by students, parents, and teachers without an onsite administrator. At its height, Creekside housed 250 students. Its small size and location were strong contributors to its family-like culture.

As a result of the discretion made possible by self-governance, teachers implemented what were then considered nontraditional practices, such as collaborative action research, collaborative examination of student work to inform practice, and multi-aged instruction. Additionally, the teachers were encouraged through their participation with the Coalition of Essential Schools (a California reform initiative) to join professional organizations such as It's Elementary! and Teacher as Researcher projects through the University of California. Subsequently, they were asked to present at educational conferences. This affirmation for developing and providing an educational program based in rigorous and relevant curriculum, and committed to the academic and social success of every child, paid unexpected dividends. As Creekside's capacity for improvement grew, so did teacher, parent, and student pride in their collective experience. "We were all learners together," said Westsmith.

Creekside's self-governance evolved over its 20-year existence. Within 5 years of opening its doors, Creekside School became the top-scoring school in the district on state standardized tests. During its 20-year tenure it continued to garner academic and social acclaim. However, despite its stellar school performance and its staff expertise in areas of curricular and leadership capacity, and in response to district declining enrollment, the Black Oak Mine Unified School District Board voted to close Creekside in June 2008.

When the school closed, Westsmith's deep democratic philosophy and her experiences at Creekside resulted in an invitation from the district and the staff of the neighboring Northside School to lead them in the shift from a principal-centered to a democratically led school. By 2015, Northside was a well-established democratic school.

Encina Preparatory High School, San Juan District, Carmichael, California. Encina Preparatory High School confronted its worst year of crisis in 2011. A school with 97% free and reduced-price lunches, 75% transiency, and 40% homelessness, its plate was already quite full. But that year, state and district funding collapsed, and the feeder middle school was closed and combined with the high school, creating Encina Preparatory High School. From 2011 to 2015, the school, spanning grades 6 through 12, had four different principals. It received teachers who had been laid off from other schools—most of whom did not want to be there. A Western Association of Schools and Colleges (WASC) team visited in 2011, but did not issue a report. They said, "We'll come back."

With the wisdom of Solomon, the district selected 10 extraordinary teachers to visit Encina and interview teachers and students. One of the teachers interviewed in 2011 was Ed Burgess, who wrote his dissertation on leadership capacity and joined the Encina staff in the fall of 2012. From this visit, five teachers were selected to head up a design team charged with creating new directions for the school. These designs were set against the backdrop of a pioneering teacher contract led by the president of the San Juan Teachers Association. Burgess points out that the significant improvements at Encina might not have occurred without the leadership of the association (personal communication, May 3–June 10, 2015).

In the late 1990s, the district had commenced extensive work in developing leadership capacity, resulting in the drafting of an adaptive policy known in the contract as Article 24. This article, entitled "Creating and Sustaining a Collaborative Culture," states: "It is the shared responsibility of the District and the Association to build the capacity of each school to function as a learning community in which professional development is job-embedded and is supported with sufficient time and resources" (San Juan Unified School District Collective Bargaining Contract, 2014, p. 91). Leadership teams were established and a continuum of emerging teacher leadership (Lambert, 2003) became one of the tools for professional development planning. The San Juan Teachers Association was a sustaining force through multiple changes in district administrative staff. Two dimensions of the new design framed and helped facilitate remarkable shifts in the culture of Encina: teacher leadership teams and the Advocacy Program. There are multiple leadership teams responsible for program areas; the school team makes decisions about everything from budgets to schedules and curriculum. The principal and one vice principal are co-equal members of the school team. More than 70% of the 58 teachers are directly involved in leading the school.

The Advocacy Program involves a 53-minute period each day in which teachers serve as advisors, counselors, and mentors to a consistent group of students. Advocacy curriculum involves preparation for college and career, assessment, problem solving, and relationship building. In order for this program to work, it was designated as one of the five teaching periods each day. Often, when such critical programs fail, it is because teachers are expected to render this valued service on top of a full teaching load.

Once avoided by parents and the community as a troubled school haunted by poor performance and violence, enrollment is now growing. The word is out that Encina is an improving and safe school. Students and families are returning.

Encina Preparatory High's achievements were made possible by significant insights and practices: (1) collaboration within the school, with the district, and with the professional association at all stages of development; (2) autonomy among and within leadership teams to allow for authority over resources and program implementation; (3) time to do the work; and (4) recruitment of the right staff by involving teacher leaders in the hiring process and the development of practitioners. In 2015, the WASC team returned, validated the school's hard work, liked what they saw, and awarded the school a full 6-year accreditation.

Maplewood Richmond Heights School District, Suburban St. Louis, Missouri. Linda Henke accepted the position of superintendent of the Maplewood Richmond Heights (MRH) School District in 2000, knowing that it was an exceptionally low-performing district, students and families were leaving the schools in droves, and halls were troubled with conflict and violence. The oldest district in the county, it had been dropping in enrollment since the 1960s; the high school had dropped from 1,100 students to below 300. There had been four superintendents in 5 years.

Early in Henke's tenure, principals and teachers were replaced, bonds proposed, and monies spent on physical plant and clean-up. At the same time, the community was mobilized. Twenty-five willing staff members met for 2 weeks the first summer of Henke's superintendency. Entitled "Dwelling in Possibilities," the extensive summer retreat included professional learning in communities, dialogue, reflection, inquiry, and leadership capacity development. Throughout the fall, 80 parents and community members met to examine the current state of affairs and discuss the community's dreams for the future. Then the climb into pride and quality began, but not before Henke was hanged in effigy in the street for her "radical" ideas.

Leadership teams guided the redesign. A new teacher evaluation system was created and professional learning time was built into the calendar. "Understanding by Design" (Wiggins & McTighe, 2005) framed the newly focused work in curriculum and instruction. K–8 looping, in which one teacher stays with the same class for more than 1 year, was implemented in the elementary school, and block scheduling at the high school. The looping and block scheduling established sustainable relationships as vital.

John Dewey's notions of democracy and experiential learning were in full bloom. Students raised chickens and bees from which they made honey. When classrooms obtained laptop computers, discipline problems dropped by 75%. The district opened "Joe's Place," a residence for homeless boys. Community activism ushered students into the streets of St. Louis to march on missions for social justice. Physically, the district became a beautiful place to learn. Color and art, sculptures, provocative poetry, and learning spaces designed to provoke creativity, including a Reggio Emilia–inspired preschool designed to function as a "studio," made MRH the pride of St. Louis.

In 2007 and 2009, the MRH Board of Education received the Education Leadership Award from the Missouri State Board of Education. By 2012, the district was awarded the top score in the state's Annual Performance Award—a perfect 100; the high school received the Apple Distinguished School Award 2 years in a row and the Follett Challenge Grand Prize.

Twelve years after she arrived, Linda Henke left behind a system that had grown slowly into one of the best districts in the country (personal communication, May 10–25, 2015).

Shared Success Elements

Creekside Elementary, Encina Preparatory High School, and the MRH District share several common elements. Each began with low student performance, disengaged staffs and communities, a lack of focus, and declining enrollment. At Encina and MRH, discipline problems and gang violence made the schools unsafe.

In two of the settings, new leaders were recruited—teachers and a principal at Encina and a superintendent in MRH—in order to move the schools in new directions. These leaders, and the existing teachers at Creekside, held a shared set of beliefs about broad-based leadership, professional learning, and the need for student support and high engagement.

- Visionary designs were initiated. At Creekside, arrangements for self-governance were planned with the district office; at Encina, a five-person design team was selected; at MRH, 80 volunteers met all summer in the first year.

- Collaborative cultures were created with teacher leadership, teams, and learning communities. Relationships took center stage.
- Leadership capacity was fostered among teachers, students, parents, and community members—and with the system as a whole.
- Adaptive policies (such as Article 24 in the San Juan district) provided flexible guidelines.
- Strong curricular and instructional foci were characterized by problem solving, critical and creative thinking, and experiential learning.
- Extraordinary and recognized progress occurred in student performance.
- Public expositions and performances took place in the form of presentations, writing, research, and applications for awards.
- Enhanced community and corporate engagement was fostered.
- Systemic change created interconnected cultures of resiliency and sustainability.

These stories, combined with scores of others in this text, reveal understandings about systemic change that hearten the learning journey. Encouraged by observed successes with leadership capacity and systems studied by the Global Fourth Way, the search for sustainability is emboldened.

SYSTEMIC CHANGE IN INTERNATIONAL SETTINGS

Around the world, educational reform is a top agenda item of many countries. While most of them are looking to national standards to specify what constitutes deeper learning for the 21st century, they are all challenged with how to implement new designs to ensure that all students learn, achieving their potential in order to be ready for college and career at the end of secondary schooling. Many countries have been involved for years in reforms they hoped would demonstrate sustainable possibilities for massive change. Few if any are satisfied with the results.

In recent years, several international programs have inspired the direction of change in the United States and elsewhere. While several nations, such as China and Korea, adopted traditional top-down approaches to teaching and learning, other countries, such as Finland, captured the imaginations of educators worldwide. Many educators in the United States and Canada realized that while archaic approaches produced individuals who could act from a predetermined set of coded instructions, few were capable of leading in the new era. Yong Zhao (2012) called this "global homogenization" (p. 31).

Yet the new millennium of knowledge creation and scientific innovation requires learners who can think and act critically and creatively, engage in entrepreneurship, perform as citizen activists, design adaptive policies, and lead. Countries at the top of the Programme for International Student Assessment (PISA) still struggle with how to help students be more creative and innovative. Policymakers and educators are continuing to experiment to determine how to know what works, when, for whom, and in what sets of circumstances.

Most of these countries understand that building the capacity of teachers to take on more responsibility for leadership, decisionmaking, research, policymaking, and innovation is a critical step. This work calls for new collaborations and interactions among and between communities and organizations in a nested system. It is possible with technology to efficiently coordinate successful, diverse paths with global impact. Education systems in Arab countries, Finland, Japan, China, Canada, Australia, Mexico, South American countries, and the United States, to name a few, are experimenting with new ways to organize their systems to meet their 21st-century learning goals. These nations expect students to learn how to learn, to inquire, to reflect, to adapt, to make decisions, and to be entrepreneurial. This is a tremendous challenge.

The five international programs described below offer approaches designed to create the conditions from which such learners emerge.

TAMAM, Arab Thought Foundation, Lebanon, Jordan, Kingdom of Saudi Arabia

A collaborative educational reform project between the American University of Beirut and the Arab Thought Foundation (ATF), TAMAM (tamamproject.org) involves selected schools, universities, and ministries in the Arab world. The ATF is an independent, nongovernmental foundation. Launched in 2007, TAMAM (an acronym for "school-based reform" in Arabic) received two grants from the ATF and a third from a private Lebanese donor. The program has expanded by adding new schools in Lebanon, Jordan, and the Kingdom of Saudi Arabia, as well as schools in Egypt, Qatar, and Oman.

Rima Karami-Akkary, the TAMAM project codirector at the American University of Beirut, described the project's approach, which analyzes the factors that enhance and hinder progress, as bottom-up change with top-down support. New prototypes of procedures were developed to create an effective road map to sustainable school-based improvement. The findings are communicated to policymakers. The program's flexible design enables it to be informed by an international knowledge base while being responsive to the local context. The program is sowing the seeds for autonomous, organically home-grown approaches and paradigms of school-based reform.

The competencies targeted for project participants include inquiry, reflective practice, collaboration, deprivatization of practice, systematic documentation of experiences, and gathering of evidence for decisionmaking. The evolving designs plan for participative leadership, mentoring, and job-embedded learning. Practitioners are coached in professional development design in order to build leadership capacity for sustainable school-based improvement. Empowered with new habits of mind, participants liberate themselves from learned passivity and become active inquirers and knowledge producers. One critical element of evidence of success involves school member participation in leading change and expanding improvement (personal communication, April 16–May 10, 2015).

A testimony from one participant:

> The project started and evolved in a way that transformed me at the personal level. I found out that its goals are not limited to school reform but have to do with building individuals who will have power to drive change starting from within their school and then the school will change within the country and then the country will drive change at the level of other countries, so it's like a blossoming rose. . . . Never before in my life have I thought that I might take part in such an experience. (TAMAM Project, 2010, p. 1)

TAMAM is supported by universities and policymakers that hope to achieve a vision of Arab schools as dynamic sources of innovation focused on student and adult learning. A regional center is being designed for research and development and to provide oversight of numerous hubs or satellites in different Arab countries. While the foundations of democracy are being built by these chosen approaches, the term *democracy* is not yet in use within the program. In September 2015, TAMAM launched its Phase Three activities, thus transforming an experimental project into a sustained movement for school-based reform in the Arab world.

The Reggio Emilia Approach, Reggio Emilia, Italy

After suffering immeasurable damage in World War II, the citizens of Reggio Emilia, Italy, began a long, creative process of developing an approach to educating young children rededicated on the best practices known at the time. As a context for research, permeated by cultural values, the Reggio Approach grew and spread internationally after *Newsweek* declared the early childhood programs there the best in the world in 1991.

In 2011, the Reggio Children–Loris Malaguzzi Centre Foundation was established to promote research in all its forms as a fundamental attitude and activity in order to improve the lives of children, families, and communities. The foundation supports policies and projects of educational, cultural, social, and scientific interest at both a national and an international level.

Julie Biddle (personal communication, May 10–11, 2015), with Antioch University, described the program. Reggio educators believe education is a right of all children and it is the responsibility of communities to ensure that all children learn. Children, they contend, are curious by nature, active citizens, and capable of constructing their own learning. Parents are co-responsible partners, and families are part of the interconnected, reciprocal relationships. The curriculum is not predetermined, but is a process of inviting and sustaining learning by creating engaging environments. Indeed, the environment is considered "the third teacher." Teachers prepare environments that are rich in materials and possibilities; they observe and listen to the children in order to know how to proceed. Using the understanding they gain, teachers then act as resources to the children by asking questions to discover children's ideas, hypotheses, and theories. Learning is viewed not as a linear process, but as a spiraling, constructivist progression. Projects provide the narrative and structure for child and adult learning alike. Pedagogical work emerges from these dynamics and is in a continuing state of change and renewal.

In international Reggio-inspired centers as well, change and innovation are welcomed. The context and cultures of each geographic region are integrated, honored, and made visible in respective interpretations. Since 1987 the United States and Canada, in collaboration with Reggio, have supported the presence of "The Hundred Languages of Children" and "The Wonder of Learning," inspiring exhibits teaching the potential of all children. Other versions of the exhibits have been displayed in Japan, New Zealand, and Israel. These inspiring exhibits make visible the potential of all children. Maplewood Richmond Heights Early Childhood Education Center and the Atwell Center for Teaching and Learning are based on the principles of the Reggio approach, while using the settings as centers for professional learning.

Professional development in the infant/toddler centers and preschool programs of Reggio Emilia is the process for understanding the methods and meanings of education through the reflective practice of observation and documentation of children in learning. Teachers-as-researchers undertake in-depth study and sharing on a daily basis and in weekly staff meetings. A *pedagogista* is assigned to several schools as a bridge between the center and the municipality and to guide professional learning. Teachers share their research and have created an international knowledge base about early childhood education. These programs exemplify the principles of professional learning described herein and capture the very essence of systems change.

Finland's School Reform

Finland's remarkable school reform efforts are undoubtedly the most thoroughly explored in the world. Country after country gained inspiration from approaches not tied to linear, controlled, test-driven goals. Responding to an internal economic crisis in the early 1970s, Finland began several stages of transformation, accelerating these approaches in the 1990s. Then, an even more constructivist plan took form in 2012–2016. The new national curriculum placed more emphasis on experiential learning, engaging learners through "phenomenon-based learning" (using science to engage with real phenomena). These approaches are built into the national curriculum.

Initially, educational transformation principles accompanied economic reforms, while adhering to strong national values: All students learn when given the opportunity and support; students are capable of driving their own learning; schools should function as democracies and provide equal, inclusive educational opportunities for all. Further, the nation holds that teachers are professional and therefore should enjoy a high degree of autonomy. The development of creativity on the part of adults and students is linked to social cohesion and economic competitiveness. These interrelated beliefs are networked throughout the country. Finland became a learning culture: Citizens participate and contribute to the collective responsibility of local democracies.

In 2000, PISA gave Finland confidence that it was on the right track with adaptive national curriculum guidelines. These guidelines allow great flexibility and autonomy at the local level. While interested in test scores, Finnish educators believe that to consider only the statistics would miss the human aspect. Actions align with beliefs: There are standardized tests only during primary and secondary schooling. As a result, while very few students (15%) score in the top-performing category, very few score in the low-performing category. This creates a collectively high average that beats the average of a country like the United States or China, countries that have gigantic educational achievement gaps mirroring their societal and economic structures (Day, 2015).

Teaching in Finland is a highly sought-after and revered career, recruiting the top 10% of high school graduates. Once an individual is selected as a teacher candidate, college is free through the acquisition of a master's degree. During formal preparation, prospective teachers are steeped in the cognitive sciences, constructivist principles, and inquiry into teaching as the primary means for professional learning.

Conditions of autonomy and support draw highly qualified individuals into a field in which they will be expected to share collective responsibility and leadership for curriculum, instruction, and assessment. Teachers learn from one another; schools learn from other schools.

A major reason Finnish students do well in school is that teachers stay with the same students for 3 to 6 years during the early phase of schooling. Consequently, teacher–student relationships are sustained through multiple grades; students are treated with respect and their learning paces are honored. This approach also helps the teachers understand the curriculum in a holistic and linear way, including a deep understanding of what students need to learn next (Hancock, 2011; Hargreaves & Shirley, 2012; Klein, 2015; Sahlberg, 2011; Zhao, 2012).

Round Square Independent Schools, United Kingdom and Greece

Founded in 1966, Round Square maintains and facilitates a worldwide network of 150 schools in 40 countries and six continents. As a not-for-profit cluster of schools, the organization is registered as a charity and governed by a board under the presidency of His Majesty King Constantine of Greece. The program was inspired by educator Kurt Hahn who founded Outward Bound and believed the greatest thing one could learn—and evoke in others—is compassion.

The network approach focuses on how learning takes place, rather than specific content. Such learning is practical, cross-cultural, and collaborative, and is infused through a broad spectrum of inter-, extra-, and co-curricular activities. Schools are provided with a structure for collaboration and the sharing of ideas. Creativity is the hallmark of the network's professional staff. Teachers lead in the development of interdisciplinary courses, forums and seminars, and international experiences. The Athenian School, described in Chapter 3, is a Round Square school. Network educators recognize the responsibility to shape the way next-generation leaders understand, prepare for, and respond to the world.

In joining the Round Square network, member schools commit to embed shared ideals throughout every learning activity within the school. They share a passion for holistic, experiential learning based on six ideals. Together, these schools seek to ensure that students achieve in ways and to levels beyond their perceived limits and expectations. The six ideals are:

- **International.** Young people are encouraged to discover and embrace the similarities and differences among cultures and nationalities in ways that promote meaningful and lasting understanding, tolerance, and respect. Students from all nationalities are welcomed and learn to see themselves as global citizens who look beyond gender, class, race, nationality, and culture to understand human nature. The schools organize term-length exchanges among students, organize students for work on essential projects in international cultures, and send delegations of students and staff to international conferences where they tackle some of the most challenging world issues through presentation, discussion, and debate.

- **Democracy.** The value of democracy and the importance of active participation in democracy are essential in Round Square schools. Forums and other channels of communication are established to enhance freedom of thought and speech. Students also are taught to appreciate self-discipline and are expected to share in the running of the school. Therefore, student government and a genuine sense of responsibility for the management of the school are goals in all schools.

- **Environment.** Students learn to tend to the future of the planet by demonstrating an active interest and concern for all natural environments, to be aware of proven problems, and to play a practical role in tackling environmental issues. A key learning point is the fine balance and the interdependence needed to maintain a healthy relationship between human beings and the planet. Special programs, work projects, and curricula all emphasize each young person's destiny to be a guardian of human society and the global environment.

- **Adventure.** Building the body and soul through adventure, meeting physical challenges, and developing an appreciation of the outdoors are all central to Round Square schools. Each school arranges outdoor and extracurricular activities that challenge and strongly engage students, individually and within groups, to promote personal growth and self-discovery. The schools also recognize that adventure is not just about the great outdoors, and that students can develop a strong spirit of adventure and inquiry through setting and then stretching to reach personal goals in areas of interest.

- **Leadership.** True leadership is found in those whose convictions are rooted in personal responsibility, kindness, and justice. Therefore, opportunities for student leadership are fostered. Leadership roles, held by senior students in particular, are substantial and range from management of housekeeping positions to holding key leadership positions. Committees in schools are chaired by students, as is the facilitation of student decisionmaking forums. The annual conference is planned and led by students.

- **Service.** A key expectation is service to others. Each student is encouraged to work a substantial number of service hours, either in school-sponsored, regional, or international projects. Round Square international service projects bring together students from member schools across the globe to work as a truly international team in some of the poorest parts of the world. The work they do is of real local value and physically demanding. Teams work in Cambodia, Peru, India, and South Africa, and tasks tackled include building and refurbishing schools, classrooms, and community centers.

The Round Square ideals described above represent "deep learning" and constitute the most desired goals for high leadership capacity and the Global Fourth Way international schools and organizations, as well as the core consensus principles fostered by the Innovative Lab Network and Declara. The following example, set in Australia, is a vivid example of Declara work.

Educational Services, Australia, and Declara, Palo Alto, California

This Australian agency, working with Declara, is tasked with supporting teachers in the implementation of communities of practice. In order to nurture and celebrate innovative practices, they created the Scootle Community, a content-rich collaboration network using big data analytics to detect patterns in teacher practices. These patterns result in recommended content and connections to support teacher self-organization and co-creation of knowledge. The Scootle Community enables all teachers in Australia to collaborate around the challenges they encountered when implementing curriculum based on the new national standards.

The next step launched a national network of design hubs in which teachers, students, experts, and community leaders can generate professional practices that promote cognitive and emotional skills. These hubs aggregate data on emerging teacher-led innovations and surface the ones that are having the greatest impact on student engagement. Teachers self-organize into different ways of collaborating. The most popular patterns of interaction involve one-to-one mentoring, small-group blogs for reflection on practice, and discussion groups. Declara supplies the platform to support collective inquiry and learning with the expectation of giving birth to a new system. Participants in these hubs report that they feel they are being treated like actual knowledge workers (González, 2014a).

CONCLUSION

At the heart of each of these international programs is a national commitment to teacher professionalism as the foundation for systems change and

21st-century student learning. Many of these programs are learning from one another—finding their reflections in the mirrors of high capacity reforms. With the advent of intelligent learning platforms and the use of design thinking to create elearning possibilities, educators everywhere are able to collaborate across schools, district, states, provinces, and nations.

As systems seek to learn from one another—and from themselves—it is wise to consider several criteria suggested in these chapters. Democratic systems liberate leadership capacity in individuals and organizations. Yet, while voice is the genesis of leadership, achieving high capacity systems requires that the breadth and skillfulness of participation be founded on a vision of social justice. Such a vision fashions healthy patterns of relationships that emerge into self-organization. And self-organization is generative; therefore it is the energy source of sustainability. These beliefs are predicated on the concept of leadership as fostering capacity through the dynamic, complex processes of purposeful, reciprocal learning.

Education systems—learning cultures—reside in a rich field of possibilities. What is known about student learning? Look to the Reggio Emilia approach and Round Square. How is professional learning best designed? Examine the Center for Teaching and Learning, New Teacher Center, and the Finnish schools. What has been learned about whole-system change? Consider leadership capacity, TAMAM, Declara, and the constructivist change processes (Figure 6.1). An array of designs and principles awaits those who are committed to building democratic societies, thus liberating leadership capacity in every learner and learning community. Each program described encompasses nearly all of the interconnected themes in this text: leadership capacity, professional learning and design thinking, the reciprocal processes of leadership, the democratization of knowledge, adaptive policies, and systemic change.

QUESTIONS FOR PERSONAL REFLECTION

1. The authors claim: "Change is a natural outcome of reciprocal human interactions in complex systems." Is this your perspective? Write out your reflections.
2. Consider a school or organization where you formerly worked. If you returned today to interview participants, which program features would you expect to find intact or adapted?
3. Are you a member of a network beyond your school? Consider the richness of networks provided by Reggio Emilia, Round Square, and Declara. What would be three advantages of joining a network?

QUESTIONS FOR GROUP REFLECTION

1. It is proposed that interventions in the domains of relationships, learning, and venue can create emergent leadership capacity features. As a group, identify three such changes to propel your school forward.
2. Is your school or organization part of a "nested system"? Describe the evidence that supports your conclusion.
3. Three examples of educational organizations are described: Creekside and Encina schools, and the Maplewood Richmond Heights School District. As individual members of your group, select three of the principles drawn from these examples to improve your own school. Compare notes and discuss.
4. Review the examples of international schools and programs described in this chapter. Which two would you most like to visit? Why?
5. Throughout this book, the authors have offered examples of programs designed to foster leadership capacity. Select two of these program descriptions you found most helpful. As a group, discuss actions to enable your schools or organizations to utilize these program strengthens and adapt them to your own settings.

Pathways to Educational Wisdom
An Epilogue

We dedicated this book to the memory of an extraordinarily wise woman: Maxine Greene. As we composed this text, we were ever mindful of two questions: What is it to be wise? Is there such a thing as a "wise school"? To be wise is different from knowing; it is different from learning and leading—although it involves all of these.

Pathways to wisdom are a journey of awakening to the possibilities and the limits of life—to the principles and responsibilities we have as humans while we reside on this "pale blue dot." Kohlberg (1994) and Gilligan, Ware, and Taylor (1988) taught us that at the higher stages of development, humans come to treasure justice, equity, and caring. These are the human gifts that enable our species to contribute to human progress and environmental sanctity—although contributions often are limited by political and religious tensions.

There is a provocative duality to wisdom. In one hand resides the humility born of insignificance as we come to understand the limits of human knowledge. In the other hand, there is the profound significance of the task of coming to understand the universes in which we reside, and thus fully participating in the drama of evolution. "The most successful people in life," argues Neil deGrasse Tyson, "recognize that they create their own love, they manufacture their own meaning, they generate their own motivation" (2012). We call it *agency*, that internal impulse to participate in this world of ours.

Such awakening, becoming aware, is a function of consciousness and was defined almost 50 years ago by Roger Sperry (1969) as an emergent quality. Throughout this text, we have discussed the nature of emergence and self-organization as enabled by networks of connectivity. The emergence of consciousness, we believe, is unleashed by the processes of constructivism.

Constructivism is a generative process that allows the imagination free rein by engaging learners with experiences and environments that provoke curiosity and generate questions, thus enabling learners to make sense of their world. The self remains intact and evolves when learners engage with ideas—curriculum content and the broader environment—yet are not subordinated to external ideas. These learners adapt what they already know and feel to the newness they encounter. Such engagement leads to discovery, for the petri dish of wisdom lies in the discrepancy between what we expect or assume and what we find to be true. Choice, discretion, reflection, discourse, inquiry, and adaptation honor the emerging learner while growing an increasingly wise individual.

These constructivist processes characterized the pathways of such able learners as Elliott Eisner, John Goodlad, Ralph Tyler, Art Costa, Wilson Riles, Bruce Joyce, and Madeline Hunter, among others (Lambert, 1983). Many held liberating metaphors for the process of learning: For Tyler, it was making love; for Costa, it meant an expanding universe; for Joyce, standing on a mountain with arms extended; for Hunter, soaring birds. Eisner was most interested in making meaning by inquiring into conceptual contexts that give forms to meaning. John Goodlad, having reached the pinnacle of his professional life at UCLA, decided to leave for Seattle. "Why?" asked his wife. "You now have everything you've wanted." "That's exactly why," Goodlad told her (personal communication, May 1982). All of these individuals were driven by an intense curiosity and restlessness, a refusal to become content with the status quo, thus lodging dissonance within themselves.

Just as constructivism can lead to wise individuals, constructivist leadership leads to wise schools. If the leadership journey we suggest is fully embarked upon, we would hope and expect to find wise schools. Maxine Greene spoke of the decency of welcoming and the desire to extend the reference of "us" as far as we can to include others. Surely these are two hallmarks of wise schools. We suggest a few additional principles:

- Stay in the conversation.
- Establish reciprocal relationships, creating co-mentors and colleagues, rather than "bosses" and "followers."
- Seek and honor diversity in all things.
- Be patient with chaos, knowing that causes are not always self-evident. When a cause is "discovered," it may be an illusion, so dig deeper, for the answers are multifaceted and often mysterious.
- Accept mutual responsibility and extend caring to the broader community.
- Set high expectations, yet know that the path to meet them is not a singular or linear one.
- Venture out rather than pulling in, letting curiosity reign; ask questions that aren't always answerable.
- Understand learning as experience that is benefited by, but not replaced by, words.
- Find and create networks.

- Realize that competition is internal; collaboration is external.
- Find the courage to say "no" if a directive is harmful to learners.
- Relinquish punishment for restoration.
- Realize that sustainability is desirable and predictive, but never a sure thing.
- Engage intellectually and emotionally every day.

As a reader, ask yourself: "Am I involved in rich conversations on a regular basis? Does my own sense of agency enable me to initiate conversations and actions that evoke wisdom in others and create a wise school?" Even though wise schools may not follow the road most traveled, believe that they are successful places for learners of all ages.

The pathways ahead flourish with possibilities. Information and knowledge are growing exponentially and becoming more and more accessible: inviting global networks, engaging social entrepreneurship, adaptive policies designed to loosen the bonds of restraint, democratic impulses struggling for air, a world population that is growing smarter through evolution, old structures collapsing into reciprocity. The moment has never been more ripe for creating the future we desire and require.

Liberating Leadership Capacity: Pathways to Educational Wisdom suggests provocative ideas, processes, and experiences designed to loosen the bonds of institutions and policies and set learning free. The context is democratic communities; the learning is constructivist; the leadership is shared. The result is wise schools, organizations, and societies.

—Linda Lambert, Diane P. Zimmerman, and Mary E. Gardner
California, 2015

References

Alper, L., Williams, K., & Hyerle, D. (2012). *Developing connective leadership: Success with thinking maps.* Bloomington, IN: Solution Tree Press.

American Educational Research Association (AERA). (2015, May). Call for knowledge and findings. Retrieved from www.aera.net/EventsMeetings/AERACentennial/CallforKnowledgeandFindings/tabid/15929/Default.aspx

Annenberg Institute for School Reform (AISR). (2004). *Professional learning communities: Professional development strategies to improve education.* Providence, RI: Brown University.

Atwell , N. (1998). *In the middle: New understandings about writing, reading, and learning* (2nd ed.). Portsmouth, NH: Heinemann.

Avolio, B. J., Walumbwa, F. O., & Weber, T. J. (2009). Leadership: Current theories, research, and future directions. *Annual Review of Psychology, 60,* 421–449.

Bandura, A. (1986). *Social foundations of thought and action: A social cognitive theory.* Englewood Cliffs, NJ: Prentice-Hall.

Bandura, A. (2001). Social cognitive theory: An agentive perspective. *Annual Review of Psychology, 52,* 1–26.

Barnes, L., Christensen, R., & Hansen, A. (1994). *Teaching and the case method* (3rd ed.). Cambridge, MA: Harvard Business School Press.

Bennett, N., Wise, C., Woods, P., & Harvey, J. (2003). Distributed leadership: A review of the literature. Nottingham, England: Open University/National College for School Leadership. Retrieved from oro.open.ac.UK/8534/1/bennett-distributed-leadership-full.pdf

Berliner, D. (1986, August–September). In pursuit of the expert pedagogue. *Educational Researcher, 15*(7), 5–13.

Blankstein, A. M. (2011). *The answer is in the room: How effective schools scale up student success.* Thousand Oaks, CA: Corwin Press.

Blankstein, A. M., Houston, P. D., & Cole, R. W. (Eds.). (2009). *Building sustainable leadership capacity.* Thousand Oaks, CA: Corwin Press.

Bohm, D. (1990). *On dialogue.* (David Bohm seminars). Ojai, CA: Bob Wilkins.

Bohm, D. (1998). *On dialogue.* New York, NY: Routledge Press.

Brafman, O., & Beckstrom, R. (2006). *The starfish and the spider: The unstoppable power of leaderless organizations.* New York, NY: Penguin Group.

Brizendine, L. (2006). *The female brain.* New York, NY: Morgan Road Books.

Brooks, D. (2014, November 14). The agency moment. *New York Times.* Retrieved from www.nytimes.com/2014/11/14/opinion/david-brooks-the-agency-moment.html

Burgess, E. F., IX. (2011). *An analysis of distributed leadership implementation in schools* (Doctoral dissertation, Walden University). Retrieved from Gradworks: Dissertation and Thesis (ATT 3487196). scholarworks.waldenu.edu/cgi/viewcontent.cgi?article=1963&context=dissertations

Burns, J. M. (1978). *Leadership.* New York, NY: Harper & Row.

Burns, J. M. (2000). Leadership and followership: Complicated relationships. In B. Kellerman & L. R. Matusak (Eds.), *Cutting edge: Leadership 2000* (pp. 10–13). College Park: James MacGregor Burns Academy of Leadership, University of Maryland.

Calkins, L. (1994). *The art of teaching writing.* Portsmouth, NH: Heinemann.

Carpenter, T., Fennema, E., Franke, M., Levi, L., & Empson, S. (2000, September). *Cognitively guided instruction: A research-based teacher professional development program in elementary school mathematics.* Madison, WI: National Center for Improving Student Learning and Achievement in Mathematics.

Chadwick, R. (2013). *Finding new ground: Beyond conflict to consensus.* Terrebonne, OR: One Tree Publishing.

Cochran-Smith, M., & Lytle, S. (1999). Relationships of knowledge and practice: Teacher learning in communities. *Review of Research in Education, 24,* 249–305.

Collay, M. (1997). The teacher as constructivist leader. In L. Lambert, M. Collay, M. Dietz, K. Kent, & A. E. Richert, *Who will save our schools? Teachers as constructivist leaders* (pp. 15–31). Thousand Oaks, CA: Corwin Press.

Collay, M. (2011). *Everyday teacher leadership: Taking action where you are.* San Francisco, CA: Jossey-Bass.

Collins, J., & Porras, J. I. (1994). *Built to last: Successful habits of visionary companies.* New York, NY: HarperCollins.

Costa, A. & Garmston, R. (2015). *Cognitive coaching: A foundation for renaissance schools* (3rd ed.). Lanham, MD: Roman & Littlefield.

Costa, A., Garmston, R., & Zimmerman, D. (2014). *Cognitive capital: Investing in teacher quality.* New York, NY: Teachers College Press.

Csikszentmihalyi, M. (2008). *Flow: The psychology of optimal experience.* New York, NY: HarperCollins.

Darling-Hammond, L. (1997). *The right to learn: A blueprint for creating schools that work.* San Francisco, CA: Jossey-Bass.

Darling-Hammond, L. (2013). *Getting teacher evaluation right: What really matters for effectiveness and improvement.* New York, NY: Teachers College Press.

Davidson, C., & Goldberg, D. (2009). *The future of learning institutions in a digital age.* Cambridge, MA: MIT Press.

Davies, B. (Ed.). (2005). *The essentials of school leadership.* London, England: Paul Chapman Publishing & Corwin Press.

Day, K. (2015). 11 ways Finland's education system shows us that "less is more". Retrieved from fillingmymap.com/2015/04/15/11-ways-finlands-education-system-shows-us-that-less-is-more/

deGrasse Tyson, N. (2012, March 1). I am Neil deGrasse Tyson. Ask me anything. Retrieved from www.reddit.com/r/IAmA/comments/qccer/i_am_neil_degrasse_tyson_ask_ me_anything/c3wgffy

Doyle, M., & Straus, D. (1976). *How to make meetings work: The new interaction method.* New York, NY: Jove.

Drago-Severson, E. (2009). *Leading adult learning: Supporting adult development in our schools.* Thousand Oaks, CA: Corwin Press.

DuFour, R., & Eaker, R. (1998). *Professional learning communities at work: Best practices for enhancing student achievement.* Bloomington, IN: Solution Tree Press.

Dweck, C. (2006). *Mindset: The new psychology of success: How we can learn to fulfill our potential.* New York, NY: Ballantine Books.

Fink, D. (2000). *Good schools/real schools: Why school reform doesn't last.* New York, NY: Teachers College Press.

Fletcher, R. (2011). *Mentor author, mentor texts: Short texts, craft notes, and practical classroom uses.* Portsmouth, NH: Heinemann.

Follett, M. P. (1924). *Creative experience.* London, England: Longsman & Green.

Forsyth, P., Adams, C., & Hoy, W. (2011). *Collective trust: Why schools can't improve without it.* New York, NY: Teachers College Press.

Freire, P. (1993). *Pedagogy of the oppressed* (M. B. Ramos, Trans.). New York, NY: Continuum. (Original work published 1970)

Fullan, M. (1998). *What's worth fighting for?* Alexandria, VA: Association for Supervision and Curriculum Development.

Fullan, M. (2005). *Leadership and sustainability: Systems thinkers in action.* Thousand Oaks, CA: Sage.

Garmston, R. (with von Frank, V.). (2012). *Unlocking group potential to improve schools.* Thousand Oaks, CA: Corwin Press.

Garmston, R., & Zimmerman, D. (2013a). The collaborative compact: Operating principles lay the foundation for group work. *Journal of Staff Development, 34*(2), 10–16.

Garmston, R., & Zimmerman, D. (2013b). *Lemons to lemonade: Resolving problems in meetings, workshops, and PLCs.* Thousand Oaks, CA: Corwin Press.

Gilligan, C., Ware, V., & Taylor, J. M. (Eds.). (1988). *Mapping the moral domain: A contribution of women's thinking to psychological theory and education.* Cambridge, MA: Harvard University Press.

Glaser, J. (2014). *Conversational intelligence: How great leaders build trust and get extraordinary results.* Brookline, MA: Bibliomotion.

Goddard, R., Hoy, W., & Woolfolk Hoy, A. (2004). Collective efficacy beliefs: Theoretical developments, empirical evidence, and future directions. *Educational Researcher, 33*(3), 3–13.

González, N. (2014a, April 17). Declara shares PD lessons from around the world. *EdSurge.* Retrieved from www.edsurge.com/news/2014-04-17-pd-lessons-from-around-the-world

González, N. (2014b). *Educators as designers: New systems to scale deep learning.* East Melbourne, VIC, Australia: Centre for Strategic Education.

Greene, M. (1995). *Releasing the imagination: Essays on education, the arts, and social change.* San Francisco, CA: Jossey-Bass.

Grimmett, P. P., & MacKinnon, A. M. (1992). Craft knowledge and the education of teachers. *Review of Research in Education, 18*, 385–456.

Hancock, L. (2011, September). Why are Finland's schools successful? *Smithsonian.* Retrieved from www.smithsonianmag.com/innovation/why-are-finlands-schools-successful-49859555/?no-ist

Hargreaves, A. (2003). *Teaching in the knowledge society: Education in the age of insecurity.* New York, NY: Teacher College Press.

Hargreaves, A. (2005). Sustaining leadership. In B. Davies (Ed.), *The essentials of school leadership* (pp. 173–189). London, England: Paul Chapman Publishing & Corwin Press.

Hargreaves, A., & Fink, D. (2006). *Sustainable leadership*. San Francisco, CA: Jossey-Bass.

Hargreaves, A., & Fullan, M. (2012). *Professional capital: Transforming teaching in every school*. New York, NY: Teachers College Press.

Hargreaves, A., & Shirley, D. (2012). *The global fourth way: The quest for educational excellence*. Thousand Oaks, CA: Corwin Press.

Harris, A. (2008). Distributed leadership through the looking glass. *Journal of Educational Administration, 46*(2). Retrieved from dx.doi.org/10.1108/jea.2008.07446baa.001

Harris, A. (2009). Against all odds: Successful leadership in challenging schools. In A. Blankstein, P. Houston, & R. Cole (Eds.), *Building sustainable leadership capacity* (pp. 85–105). Thousand Oaks, CA: Corwin Press.

Heifetz, R. A. (1994). *Leadership without easy answers*. Cambridge, MA: Harvard University Press.

Heifetz, R. A., Grashow, A., & Linsky, M. (2009). *The practice of adaptive leadership: Tools and tactics for changing your organization and the world*. Boston, MA: Harvard Business Press.

Hiebert, J., Gallimore, R., & Stigler, J. (2002). A knowledge base for the teaching profession: What would it look like and how do we get one? *Educational Researcher, 31*(5), 3–15.

Hord, S. (1997). *Professional learning communities: Communities of continuous inquiry and improvement*. Austin, TX: Southwest Educational Development Laboratory.

Huberman, M. (1989). The professional life cycle of teachers. *Teachers College Record, 91*(1), 31–57.

Humme, A. (2012, December 10). *Education is a human right!* Retrieved from www.globalpartnership.org/blog/education-human-right

Immordino-Yang, M. (2008). Emotions, social relationships, and the brain: Implications for classrooms. *ASCD Express, 3*(20). Retrieved from www.ascd.org/ascd_express/vol3/320_immordino-yang.aspx

Immordino-Yang, M. H., & Damasio, A. (2007). We feel, therefore we learn: The relevance of affective and social neuroscience to education. *Mind, Brain, and Education, 1*(1), 3–10.

Isaacs, W. (1999). *Dialogue and the art of thinking together*. New York, NY: Doubleday.

Jago, C. (2002). *Cohesive writing: Why concept is not enough*. Portsmouth, NH: Heinemann.

Johnston, P., & Goatley, V. (December 2014/January 2015). Research making its way into classroom practice. *The Reading Teacher, 68*(4). doi: 10.1002/trtr.1278

Jones, S., Harvey, M., Lefoe, G., Ryland, K. (2014). Synthesising theory and practice: Distributed leadership in higher education. *Educational Management Administration & Leadership, 42*(5), 603–619. Retrieved from ema.sagepub.com/content/early/2014/02/11/1741143213510506?papetoc

Kegan, R. (1982). *The evolving self: Problems and process in human development*. Cambridge, MA: Harvard University Press.

Kegan, R. (1994). *In over our heads: The mental demands of modern life.* Cambridge, MA: Harvard University Press.

Kegan, R., & Lahey, L. (2009). *Immunity to change: How to overcome it and unlock the potential in yourself and your organization.* Boston, MA: Harvard Business School Press.

Kellerman, B. (2008). *Followership: How followers are creating change and changing leaders.* Boston, MA: Harvard Business School Press.

Kellerman, B. (2012). *The end of leadership.* New York, NY: HarperCollins.

Kelley, T., & Kelley, D. (2013). *Creative confidence: Unleashing the creative potential within us all.* London, England: William Collins.

King, A. J., Johnson, D. P., & Van Vugt, M. (2009, October). The origins and evolution of leadership. *Current Biology, 19,* R911–R916.

Klein, R. (2015, March 28). Finland's schools are overhauling the way they do things. Here's how. *The Huffington Post.* Retrieved from www.huffingtonpost .com/2015/03/28/finland-education- overhaul_n_6958786.html

Kocolowski, M. (2010). *Shared leadership: Is it time for a change?* Virginia Beach, VA: Regents Press.

Kohlberg, L. (1994). *The psychology of moral development.* San Francisco, CA: Harper & Row.

Korgerus, M., & Tschappeler, R. (2011). *The decision book: 50 models for strategic thinking* (J. Piening, Trans.). New York, NY: Norton.

Krovetz, M., & Arriaza, G. (2006). *Collaborative teacher leadership: How teachers can foster equitable schools.* Thousand Oaks, CA: Corwin Press.

Lambert, L. (1983). *A critical analysis of the assumptions held by policy makers, staff developers, and writers about adult learning* (Unpublished doctoral dissertation). University of San Francisco, San Francisco, CA.

Lambert, L. (1988, May). Staff development redesigned. *Phi Delta Kappan, 69*(9), 665–668.

Lambert, L. (1998). *Building leadership capacity in schools.* Alexandria, VA: ASCD.

Lambert, L. (2003). *Leadership capacity for lasting school improvement.* Alexandria, VA: ASCD.

Lambert, L. (2005). Constructivist leadership. In B. Davies (Ed.), *The essentials of school leadership* (pp. 93–109). London, England: Paul Chapman Publishing & Corwin Press.

Lambert, L. (2009). Reconceptualizing the road toward leadership capacity. In A. Blankstein, P. Houston, & R. Cole (Eds.), *Building sustainable leadership capacity* (pp. 7–28). Thousand Oaks, CA: Corwin Press.

Lambert, L., Collay, M., Dietz, M. E., Kent, K., & Richert, A. E. (1997). *Who will save our schools? Teachers as constructivist leaders.* Thousand Oaks, CA: Corwin Press.

Lambert, L., & Gardner, M. E. (2009). *Women's ways of leading.* Indianapolis, IN: Dog Ear Press.

Lambert, L., Walker, D., Zimmerman, D., Cooper, J., Lambert, M., Gardner, M., & Ford Slack, P. (1995). *The constructivist leader.* New York, NY: Teachers College Press.

Lambert, L., Walker, D., Zimmerman, D., Cooper, J., Lambert, M., Gardner, M., & Szabo, M. (2002). *The constructivist leader* (2nd ed.). New York, NY: Teachers College Press.

Lave, J., & Wenger, E. (1991). *Situated learning: Legitimate peripheral participation,* Cambridge, England: Cambridge University Press.

Learning Forward. (2015, December 10). ESSA includes improved definition of professional development [press release]. Retrieved from learningforward.org /who-we-are/announcements/press-releases/2015/12/10/essa-includes -improved-definition-of-professional-development#.Vpl3aVJ8ldw

Leithwood, K., & Jantzi, D. (2005). A review of transformational school leadership research 1996–2005. *Leadership and Policy in Schools, 4*(3), 177–199.

Levine, S. L. (1989). *Promoting adult growth in schools: The promise of professional development.* Boston, MA: Allyn & Bacon.

Lieberman, A. (1995). Practices that support teacher development: Transforming conceptions of professional learning. *Phi Delta Kappan, 76,* 591–596.

Lieberman, A., & Miller, L. (1991). *Staff development for education in the '90s: New demands, new realities, new perspectives.* New York, NY: Teachers College Press.

Louis, K. S. (2007). Trust and improvement in schools. *Journal of Educational Change, 8*(1), 1–24.

Louis, K. S., Leithwood, K., Wahlstrom, K., Anderson, S., Michlin, M., Mascall, B., & Moore, S. (2010). *Learning from leadership: Investigating the links to improved student learning.* Retrieved from www.wallacefoundation.org/Pages /acknowledgments-learning-from-leadership.aspx

Loucks, S. F., & Hall, G. E. (1979, April 12). Implementing innovations in schools: A concerns-based approach. Paper presented at AERA conference, San Francisco, CA.

Marion, R. (1999). *The edge of organization: Chaos and complexity theories of formal social organizations.* Newbury Park, CA: Sage.

Martin, R., & Osberg, S. (2007, Spring). Social entrepreneurship: The case for definition. *Stanford Social Innovation Review,* pp. 29–39. Retrieved from www. ssir. org/articles/entry/social_entrepreneurship_the_case_for_definition

McKelvey, B. (2001). Energizing order-creating networks of distributed intelligence. *International Journal of Innovation Management, 5,* 181–212.

McLoughlin, C., & Lee, M. (2010). Personalised and self regulated learning in the Web 2.0 era: International exemplars of innovative pedagogy using social software. *Australasian Journal of Educational Technology, 26*(1), 28–43.

Moller, G., & Pankake, A. (2006). *Lead with me: A principal's guide to teacher leadership.* London, England: Routledge.

Morones, A. (2014, March 5). Teachers lead the way in Nevada leader's Common-Core project. *Education Week.* Retrieved from www.edweek.org/ew /articles/2014/03/05/23ltlf-grossman.h33.html

National School Reform Faculty (NSRF). (2014). Mission. Retrieved from www .nsrfharmony.org/about-us/mission-statement

Nepo, M. (2012). *Seven thousand ways to listen: Staying close to what is sacred.* New York, NY: Free Press.

Ogawa, R. T. (2005). Leadership as a social construct: The expression of human agency within organizational constraint. In F. W. English (Ed.), *The Sage handbook of educational leadership: Advances in theory, research, and practice* (pp. 89–108). Thousand Oaks, CA: Sage.

Ormandale Elementary School. (2008). *A guide to investigative learning.* Retrieved from www.pvsd.net/page/103

Palmer, P. (1998). *The courage to teach: Exploring the inner landscapes of a teacher's life.* San Francisco, CA: Jossey-Bass.

Pentland, A. (2014). *Social physics: How good ideas spread—the lessons from a new science.* New York, NY: Penguin Press.

Pink, D. H. (2005). *A whole new mind: Moving from the information age to the conceptual age.* New York, NY: Riverhead Books.

Pomerantz, F., & Ippolito, J. (2015, February). Power tools for conversations: Custom protocols enrich coaching conversations. *Journal of Staff Development, 36*(1), 40–43.

Queensland Brain Institute. (2014). *Major projects: Attention and the readiness for action.* Retrieved from www.cunningtonlab.net

Richardson, V., & Placier, P. (2001). Teacher change. In V. Richardson (Ed.), *Handbook of research on teaching* (4th ed., pp. 905–947). Washington, DC: American Educational Research Association.

Robb, L. (2010). *Teaching middle school writers: What every English teacher needs to know.* Portsmouth, NH: Heinemann.

Rowe, M. B. (1986). Wait time: Slowing down may be a way of speeding up! *Journal of Teacher Education, 37*(1), 43–50.

Ruttonsha, P., & Quilley, S. (2014). *The many faces of design: From adaptive response to creative agency to immersive engagement.* Retrieved from www.academia.edu/15458125/The_Many_Faces_of_Design_From_Adaptive_Response_to_Creative_Agency_to_Immersive_Engagement

Sahlberg, P. (2011). *Finnish lessons: What can the world learn from educational change in Finland.* New York, NY: Teachers College Press.

San Juan Unified School District Collective Bargaining Contract. (2014). Carmicheal, CA. Retrieved from www.sanjuan.edu/cms/lib8/CA01902727/Centricity/Domain/4377/sjta_contract_1214.pdf

Sandberg, S. (2015, March 5). How men can succeed in the boardroom and the bedroom. *New York Times.* Retrieved from www.nytimes.com/2015/03/08/opinion/sunday/sheryl-sandberg-adam-grant-how-men-can-succeed-in-the-boardroom-and-the-bedroom.html

Schein, E. (1993). On dialogue, culture, and organizational learning. *Organizational Dynamics, 22*(2), 40–51.

Schoenfield, A. (2006). What doesn't work: The challenge and the failure of the What Works Clearinghouse to conduct meaningful review of the studies of mathematics curricula. *Educational Researcher, 35*(6), 15–21.

Schon, D. A. (1983). *The reflective practitioner: How professionals think in action.* New York, NY: Basic Books.

School Reform Initiative. (2016). Protocols. Retrieved from www.schoolreforminitiative.org/protocols/

Senge, P., Scharmer, C. O., Jaworski, J., & Flowers, B. S. (2004). *Presence.* New York, NY: Doubleday.

Shanahan, T. (2015, April 5). Response to complaint about What Works Clearinghouse [blog post]. Retrieved from www.shanahanonliteracy.com/2015/04/response-to-complaint-about-what-works.html

Shannon, G. S., & Bylsma, P. (2007). *Nine characteristics of high-performing schools: A research-based resource for schools and districts to assist with improving learning* (2nd ed.). Olympia, WA: Office of Superintendent of Public Instruction.

Slavin, R. (2007, December 18). The What Works Clearinghouse: Time for a fresh start. *Education Week*. Retrieved from www.edweek.org/ew/articles/2007/12/19/16slavin.h27.html

Smith, C. (2014, September). *Developing teacher leaders for social justice: Building agency through community, critical reflection, and action research* (Doctoral dissertation, University of Manitoba). Retrieved from hdl.handle.net/1993/23995

Smith, M. K. (2003, 2009). Jean Lave, Etienne Wenger and communities of practice. *Encyclopedia of Informal Education*. Retrieved from www.infed.org/biblio/communities_of_practice.htm

Snow-Gerono, J. (2005). Professional development in a culture of inquiry: PDS teachers identify the benefits of professional learning communities. *Teaching and Teacher Education, 21*, 241–256.

Southworth, G. (2005). Learner-centred leadership. In B. Davies (Ed.), *The essentials of school leadership* (pp.75–92). London, England: Paul Chapman Publishing & Corwin Press.

Sperry, R. W. (1969). A modified concept of consciousness. *Psychological Review, 76*(6), 532–536.

Spillane, J. P. (2002). *Distributed leadership*. San Francisco, CA: Jossey-Bass.

Spillane, J. P., Camburn, E. M., Pustejovsky, J., Pareja, A. S., & Lewis, G. (2006, April). Taking a distributed perspective: Epistemological and methodological trade-offs in operationalizing the leader-plus aspect. Paper presented at the Annual meeting of the American Educational Research Association, San Francisco, CA, April 7–11, 2006.

Spillane, J. P., Halverson, R., & Diamond, J. B. (2004). Distributed leadership: Toward a theory of school leadership practice. *Journal of Curriculum Studies, 36*(1), 3–34.

Stoll, L., & Jackson, D. (2009). Liberating leadership potential: Designing for leadership capacity. In A. Blankstein, P. Houston, & R. Cole (Eds.), *Building sustainable leadership capacity* (pp. 65–84).Thousand Oaks, CA: Corwin Press.

Stoll, L., Rolam, R., McMahon, A., Wallace, M., & Thomas, S. (2006, Spring). Professional learning communities: A review of the literature. *Journal of Educational Change, 7*, 221–258.

Swanson, D., Barg, S., Tyler, S., Venema, H. D., Tomar, S., Bhadwal, S., . . . & Drexhage, J. (2009). Seven guidelines for policy-making in an uncertain world. In D. Swanson, & S. Bhadwal (Eds.), *Creating adaptive policies: A guide for policy-making in an uncertain world* (pp. 12–24). New Delhi, India: Sage.

Sylwester, R., & Cho. J. (December 1992/January, 1993). What brain research says about paying attention. *Educational Leadership. 50*(4), 71–75.

TAMAM Project. (2010). A school-based reform project for the Arab world. Retrieved from www.tamamproject.org/the_professional_development_program.html

Taylor, G. (2015). Libraries and museums. Retrieved from www.tomorrowmakers.org/articles-resources/

Taylor, G., & Johnston, T. (2009). From hierarchy to panarchy: The unfolding of a global paradigm shift (Version 4.2). San Francisco, CA: Creative Commons. Retrieved from www.tomorrowmakers.org/articles-resources/

Thomas, D., & Brown, J. S. (2011). *A new culture of learning: Cultivating the imagination for a world of constant change*. CreateSpace.

Thomas, D., & Brown, J. S. (2012, February 27). New models of learning, new models of engagement—Cultivating resilient learners, designers and researchers for the 21st century. Presentation given at DeLange Conference VIII: The Future of the Research University, Rice University, Houston, Texas. February 27, 2012. Retrieved from johnseelybrown.com/delange.pdf

Uhl-Bien, M., & Marion, R. (2008). Complexity leadership—A framework for leadership in the twenty-first century. In M. Uhl-Bien & R. Marion (Eds.), *Complexity leadership: Part 1. Conceptual foundation* (pp. xi–xxiv). Charlotte, NC: Information Age.

Uhl-Bien, M., Marion, R., & McKelvey, B. (2007). Complexity leadership theory: Shifting leadership from the industrial age to the knowledge era. *Leadership Institute Faculty Publications,* Paper 18. Retrieved from digitalcommons.unl.edu/leadershipfacpub/18

Venema, H., & Drexhage, J. (2009). The need for adaptive policies. In D. Swanson & S. Bhadwal (Eds.), *Creating adaptive policies*: *A guide for policy-making in an uncertain world* (pp. 1–11). New Delhi, India: Sage.

Weingarten, R. (2015, July 19). The power of collective voice. *The Huffington Post.* Retrieved from www.huffingtonpost.com/randi-weingarten/the-power-of-collective-v_b_7827116.html

Wenger, E. (1998). *Communities of practice: Learning, meaning, and identity.* Cambridge, England: Cambridge University Press.

Westsmith, W. (2014). *Leading from within—Northside school: A study of shared leadership.* (Unpublished doctoral dissertation). Saint Mary's College of California, Moraga.

Wheatley, M. (1992). *Leadership and the new sciences.* Oakland, CA: Berrett-Koehler.

Wiggins, G., & McTighe, J. (2005). *Understanding by design.* Alexandria, VA: Association for Supervision and Curriculum Development.

Wood Ray, K. (1999). *Wondrous words: Writers and writing in the elementary classroom.* Urbana, IL: National Council of English Teachers.

'World's best teacher' does not believe in tests and quizzes. (2015, April 29). *PBS Newshour.* Retrieved from www.pbs.org/newshour/bb/worlds-best-teacher-believe-tests-quizzes/

Yenawine, P. (2013). *Visual thinking strategies: Using art to deepen learning across school disciplines.* Cambridge, MA: Harvard Education Press.

York-Barr, J., Sommers, W., Chere, G., & Montie, J. (2006). *Reflective practice to improve schools: An action guide for educators* (2nd ed.). Thousand Oaks, CA: Corwin Press.

Zhao, Y. (2012). *World class learners: Educating creative and entrepreneurial students.* Thousand Oaks, CA: Corwin Press.

Index

About the Authors

Linda Lambert, EdD, is professor emeritus at California State University, East Bay, and president of Lambert Leadership Development. She has served in multiple leadership roles, including principal, district administrator, director of reform initiatives, and consultant at local, state, national, and international levels. Her pioneering work in leadership led to invitations from the U.S. State Department and foreign ministries to consult in Thailand, Australia, Malaysia, Singapore, Canada, Great Britain, Mexico, Lebanon, and, most extensively, Egypt. Her work has been translated into Chinese, Malay, Hebrew, Lithuanian, and Spanish. Major consulting and research foci include constructivist leadership, leadership capacity, women in leadership, and organizational development. In addition to dozens of articles and book chapters, Linda is the lead author of *The Constructivist Leader* (1995, 2002), *Who Will Save Our Schools?* (1997), and *Women's Ways of Leading* (2009). She is the author of *Building Leadership Capacity in Schools* (1998), *Leadership Capacity for Lasting School Improvement* (2003), and three novels known as The Justine Trilogy. The first novel, *The Cairo Codex*, won a Nautilus and an Independent Book Sellers award for best fiction. Other awards include International Book of the Year (*The Constructivist Leader*, 1997), Outstanding California Educator, and Professor of the Year. She lives in Santa Rosa, California, with her husband, Morgan Lambert.

Diane P. Zimmerman, PhD, recently retired as a superintendent of schools, after a 36-year career in public education. Diane is a writer and consultant focusing on building human capacity. She is a skilled Cognitive Coach with expertise in facilitation, conflict management, and leadership development. Diane has coauthored two books with Art Costa and Robert Garmston and is a coauthor of *The Constructivist Leader* (1995, 2002). She has written a wide variety of articles and chapters about communication, leadership development, and school change, and her journal articles regularly appear in the *Journal of Staff Development*. In 1998 she obtained her PhD in human and organizational development from the Fielding Graduate Institute. She has taught college courses at Sacramento State University and Sonoma State University.

Throughout her career, Diane has been involved in handling divergent opinions and mediating conflict. She has proven she can work with staff and community to develop creative talents. In her years as a principal and superintendent she invested in staff by fostering talents and leadership capacity. She takes great pride in being part of communities that not only work well together, but also seek challenges as an opportunity for learning and knowledge development. Diane lives in Suisun Valley, California, with her husband, Rich Zimmerman.

Mary E. Gardner, MA, is a retired school district superintendent and has been an educational leader, lecturer, and consultant for more than 40 years. While in graduate school at UC Berkeley, she was a research assistant to Anne Dyson and authored articles on early literacy. She is also a coauthor of *The Constructivist Leader* (1995, 2002) and *Women's Ways of Leading* (2009). Mary was an invited visiting practitioner at Harvard University in 1988–1989. She taught educational leadership at California State University, East Bay, and San Jose State University. She has continued to influence the field of women's leadership, organizational development, and literacy. Her multimedia workshops, seminars, and keynote speeches have placed her in demand as an exemplary woman leader. Mary's remarkable contributions have been acknowledged through awards such as Soroptimist's Women of Distinction and California school administrators' Women of the Year. She has served on five nonprofit boards. Mary lives in San Jose, California.